Letts

Framework FOCUS

101 Red Hot English Starters

Simon Adorian
Beth Brooke
Lyn Gaudreau

Contents

About the authors

Simon Adorian is an experienced English teacher and is currently Deputy Headteacher of a large 9–13 Middle School. He has worked as an LEA Literacy Consultant and is a respected published writer of plays for schools.

Beth Brooke is an LEA KS3 English Consultant. She previously taught English at both KS2 and KS3 and has published work on using literacy in the history curriculum.

Lyn Gaudreau is an LEA KS3 English Consultant. She was previously a Head of English in secondary schools.

Acknowledgements

The publishers would like to thank the following for permission to use copyright material. Every effort has been made to trace copyright holders and to obtain their permission for the use of copyright material. The author and publishers will gladly receive information enabling them to rectify any error or omission in subsequent editions.

© Bill Bryson. Extracted from NOTES FROM A SMALL ISLAND, published by Transworld Publishers, a division of the Random House Group Ltd. All rights reserved.

MOTHER TONGUE: THE ENGLISH LANGUAGE by Bill Bryson (Hamish Hamilton, 1990) Copyright © Bill Bryson, 1990.

HAPPY DAYS WITH THE NAKED CHEF by Jamie Oliver (Michael Joseph, 2001) Copyright © Jamie Oliver, 2001.

MORE STORIES JULIAN TELLS by Ann Cameron (Harper Collins, 1987) Copyright © Ann Cameron, 1987.

Introduction

Introducing starters

An effective lesson will often begin with an activity that is interactive, pacy and engaging. The Key Stage 3 *Framework for Teaching English* acknowledges that a starter activity, as introduction to the three-part lesson, is an ideal way of grabbing the group's attention in an engaging and challenging way.

This book contains a collection of lesson starters encompassing a variety of teaching and learning activities: quizzes, pencil and paper activities, role-plays and games are all included. Most of them require very few resources.

Target audience

The book is mainly intended for use in Key Stage 3 English lessons. It will hopefully offer teachers ways of tackling objectives from the *Framework for Teaching English* (especially some of the trickier aspects of spelling and grammar) in an enjoyable and interactive style. However, most of the activities would also be effective with older or younger students.

Using starters

These starters are designed to be short, sharp activities that focus explicitly on one or two objectives. They are intended to be flexible and clearly need to be used in the context of what the class is learning at the moment. They can be used for two main teaching purposes:

- to 'soften up' students for the main objective of the lesson or unit of work

- to consolidate and refresh memories by applying previous knowledge in a way that is more appealing and motivating than the traditional classroom written exercise.

In other words, these starter activities are meant to be a complement to your teaching of Framework objectives and not to be a complete course in themselves. They will not teach all your Literacy objectives for you, but they should help to bring your students 'in the zone'.

Where suitable, we have included follow-up suggestions that hint at ways in which a sequence of further activities can be developed. Some of the starter activities can be broken down for use over two or three lessons. They could also be used in plenaries to round up the lesson and establish what has been understood. A brisk game might be useful to revive flagging concentration at the end of a lesson.

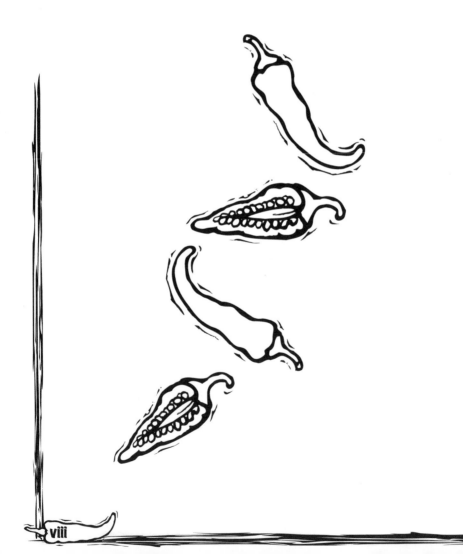

How to use this book

Contents grid

For simplicity, each starter has been assigned to one specific year group and one or two objectives only. However, all the activities are extremely flexible. Most of them can be used for any Key Stage 3 year group and adapted according to your students' abilities. In reality, the activities also often cover more objectives.

Objectives

Each starter activity has been matched to one or two appropriate Key Stage 3 objectives and an aim is clearly stated. Underpinning the whole book is a wish to develop students' enjoyment of playing with words, and of taking on sentence structures or writing styles and trying them out for size. Our experience is that a word game using individual whiteboards and pens can be less daunting than a blank page.

Resources

Most of the starters require nothing more than pencil and paper or individual whiteboards and pens, and they are light on preparation and photocopying.

Activities

Each starter opens with one or two learning objectives, followed by the aims of the activity. The activity is outlined using concise bulleted action points, and examples and ideas for modelling have been suggested where appropriate.

Differentiation

In some cases, specific ideas are offered for modifying the activities: the up arrow ⇑ shows how to make the starter more challenging; the down arrow ⇓ indicates how to support less confident students. However, the majority of activities are designed for use with groups of mixed ability students and most of them can be presented as games or open-ended challenges. Many can be tackled in pairs, groups or teams where students can support one another.

The starters in this book have been tried and tested with a variety of classes, of differing abilities, so they certainly do work. It is important, however, that you adapt and modify the activities to suit the needs of your classes and sometimes this needs a little perseverance and patience. Whichever way you choose to use them, we are sure that your students will find them satisfying and fun whilst improving their mastery over language.

Simon Adorian, Beth Brooke, Lyn Gaudreau

Same sound, different letters

Objective covered
W1 *Correct vowel choices, including vowels with common alternative spellings, e.g. 'ay', 'ai', 'a_e'.*

Aim
To investigate the choices for spelling long vowel sounds.

Activity
- Ask the students to work in pairs or teams. How many English words can they find which spell the long 'ay' sound differently? Some examples are:

  - a_e → gate
  - ai → rain
  - ay → tray
  - ey → grey
  - eig → reign
  - eigh → weight
  - aigh → straight
  - ea → great
  - ei → rein
  - a → able
  - ag → champagne
  - e_e → fete

- The same challenge can be set for all the long vowel sounds.

Follow up
- A variation on this is 'Same letter(s), different sounds'. Ask the students to spell six or seven different English words containing the letter string '-ough' where the '-ough' makes a different sound/phoneme. For example:

cough	(-off)	bough	(-ow)
rough	(-uff)	thought	(-aw)
though	(-o)	lough	(this a bit of a cheat – in Northern Ireland it is pronounced 'loch')
thorough	(unstressed -uh)		

...wel choices

Objective covered

W1 *Correct vowel choices, including vowels with common alternative spellings, e.g. 'ay', 'ai', 'a_e'.*

Aim

To investigate the choices for spelling long vowel sounds.

Resources

Computers with word-processing programs.

Activity

- ✸ This activity is an ideal starter to a lesson scheduled in an ICT suite. It can be applied to all spelling choices, for example **W3** *Making choices between similar endings such as '-cian', '-sion' and '-tion'.*

- ✸ Tell the students you are going to dictate 10 words for them to key in.

- ✸ Dictate these 10 words which have the same vowel sound (long 'a'):

  chain, fail, rage, brain, fate, stray, straight, day, reign, grey.

- ✸ Students should then use a spellchecker to check them.

- ✸ Draw the students' attention to the variety of letter strings (graphemes) representing the same sound. Some choices are more commonly used than others.

Follow up

- ✸ Ask the students to combine all 10 words into an interesting text on the screen, using as few additional words as possible. Different forms (e.g. tenses, plurals) can be used. What is the smallest number of words that can be used? For example: 'The last day of his reign was grey. As a rage overcame his brain, he failed to pull the chain straight and fate caused him to stray.'

Millionaire plurals

Objective covered / aim

W2 *Pluralisation, including '-es' endings and words ending in 'y', 'f' and vowels.*

Activity

- ✦ Play *Who Wants To Be A Millionaire?*
- ✦ Choose a different volunteer for each step of the game. No one can be in the chair for more than one question (save better spellers for the higher stakes).
- ✦ For each step, the student on the spot is given the singular form of a noun (written on the board). They are then offered the board pen/chalk to spell the plural form of the noun.
- ✦ Three lifelines are allowed:
  - ask the audience (offer answers for a class vote)
  - phone a friend (the student on the spot can ask someone else to spell the word)
  - 50/50 (offer the student two choices).
- ✦ Use lists of nouns with increasingly challenging plurals. Have alternatives for the first stages, so that an early failure can be quickly followed up. Two full lists are supplied below.

£100	face	(faces)	house	(houses)
£200	watch	(watches)	dish	(dishes)
£300	sheep	(sheep)	foot	(feet)
£500	woman	(women)	knife	(knives)
£1000	monkey	(monkeys)	donkey	(donkeys)
£2000	family	(families)	penny	(pennies)
£4000	scarf	(scarves)	loaf	(loaves)
£8000	louse	(lice)	mouse	(mice)
£16 000	goose	(geese)	tooth	(teeth)
£32 000	potato	(potatoes)	buffalo	(buffaloes)
£64 000	antenna	(antennae)	larva	(larvae)
£125 000	quiz	(quizzes)	walrus	(walruses)
£500 000	banjo	(banjos)	crisis	(crises)
£1 000 000	ox	(oxen)	stimulus	(stimuli)

That's the end

Objective covered/aim

W3 *Word endings, including vowel suffixes such as '-ing'; consonant suffixes such as '-ful'; modifying words ending in 'y' or 'e'; making choices between similar endings such as '-cian', '-sion' and '-tion'.*

Resources

Individual whiteboards and pens.

Activity

⊛ Choose a particular word ending, for example '-tting'. Display this on the board. The students now have three minutes to see how many words they can find ending in those letters.

⊛ At the end of the time, ask the students to show their whiteboards and see who has found the most words. Look out for incorrect spellings. Collect observations about the kind of words that end in this way. In the case of '-tting', the double consonant means the letters can only follow a short vowel.

⊛ Other useful endings to use include:

-nning, -lling,	-cian, -sion, -tion	-or
-pping	-ches, -ces, -zes	-ous, -us
-mmed, -lled, -tted	-ries, -eys	-cal, -mal
-ning, -ring, -ting	-ble	-ance, -ence
-ful, -iful	-lly	-ure

Differentiation

⊛ ⇓ Less confident spellers could play this game in a small group using a pack of cards with selected word endings. When an ending is chosen, each student takes it in turns to spell a word ending that way.

⊛ ⇑ More confident spellers could play in pairs against each other. One player specifies a word ending and then the first one to write ten words scores a point. Next time round the other player calls the ending.

Spelling team challenge

Objective covered / aim

W3 *Word endings, including vowel suffixes such as '-ing'; consonant suffixes such as '-ful'; modifying words ending in 'y' or 'e'; making choices between similar endings such as '-cian', '-sion' and '-tion'.*

Resources

Individual whiteboards and pens.

Activity

⊛ This team game can be played to revise any spelling pattern. It is designed to keep as many players involved as possible.

⊛ Remind the class of the spelling pattern to be covered, for example 'shun' endings. Revise some of the key principles or the main spelling choices involved, for example '-cian', '-sion', '-tion'.

⊛ Divide the group into two teams. Give every player on each team a number. Opposite numbers need to be well matched.

⊛ The game is played as follows:

- Everyone has two minutes to write on one side of their board a number of words that fit the spelling pattern. They are aiming to write words that they can spell but that their opposite number might not be able to spell.

- After two minutes call out a number, for example 'Number 7'.

- The 'Number 7' on one team then has to call out one of the words on their board.

- Everyone in the room has a go at spelling the word on the other side of their whiteboard.

- Now ask 'Number 7' on the opposing team to show their attempt. If it is correct, that side scores a point.

- If the word is incorrectly spelt, the player who set the challenge shows their version of the word. If correct, their team scores a point.

Human words

Objectives covered

W3 *Word endings*
W4 *Prefixes, including antonym prefixes, e.g. 'ir-', 'un-'.*

Aim

To experiment with combining morphemes to make whole words.

Resources

Individual whiteboards and pens.

Activity

- ✷ Split the class into three equal groups: 'prefixes', 'roots' and 'suffixes'.
- ✷ Write Table 1 on the board. You need to shuffle the word parts as the table below shows the answer.

Table 1			Table 2		
Prefix	**Root**	**Suffix**	**Prefix**	**Root**	**Suffix**
con	vince	ing	con	script	ion
under	achieve	er	dis	hearten	ing
dis	appear	ance	de	cept	ive
re	call	ed	re	peat	ition
pre	dict	ion	un	music	al
de	compose	ition	im	poss	ible
non	sense	ical	in	cure	able
inter	nation	al	sub	miss	ion
un	happy	ness	trans	form	ation
in	access	ible	super	intend	ent

- ✷ Allocate each member of each group a word part to copy onto their individual whiteboard.
- ✷ Students now have to get into groups of three so that they form words. This will need simple modelling first, for example: 'un-help-ful'. You will also need to show how some root words ending in '-e' and '-y' have to be modified, for example: 'un-believe-able'.
- ✷ There are many possible combinations but only the ones above use up all the word parts.
- ✷ Repeat using the Table 2. Note the unusual modification of the root in 'repetition'.

Wordbuilding

Objectives covered

W3 *Word endings, including vowel suffixes such as '-ing'; consonant suffixes such as '-ful'; modifying words ending in 'y' or 'e'; making choices between similar endings such as '-cian', '-sion' and '-tion'.*
W4 *Prefixes, including antonym prefixes, e.g. 'ir-', 'un-'.*

Aim

To investigate affixes.

Activity

⊛ This is a game that can be played by individuals, pairs or teams.

⊛ Call out a root from the list below. Give the students a fixed time to come up with the longest word containing that root. For example: 'finite' could lead to 'infinity', 'definition', 'infinitesimal'; 'form' could lead to 'reformers', 'reformation', 'deformities'.

⊛ The scoring system is as follows:
  • 1 point for adding before the root (prefixes)
  • 1 point for adding after the root (suffixes)
  • 1 point if the word is a real word
  • 2 points for the student/team with the longest word.
  Points could also be awarded for successful 'challenges' to invented words.

⊛ Suitable roots for the game are:

form	finite	cycle	press
cept	port	script	nation
pose	medic	spect	fect

Follow up

⊛ Ask students to use a dictionary to find other roots for the game. They will need to look for long words beginning with common prefixes, such as 'in-', 're-', 'dis-'.

1, 2, 3, 4

Objective covered
W4 *Prefixes, including antonym prefixes, e.g. 'ir-', 'un-'.*

Aim
To investigate words using number prefixes.

Resources
Dictionaries.

Activity
⊛ Display this table:

Prefix	Number	Example
uni	one	unicycle
bi/duo	two	bilingual/duet
tri	three	triangle
quad/quart	four	quadrangle/quartet
dec	ten	decade

⊛ Ask the students to use dictionaries to see how many words they can find with different number prefixes.

Hint
⊛ The clues for these words lie in their meaning as well as their spelling. Although not every word beginning with the letters 'bi' is using a number prefix, the spelling of some words gives a clue to their etymology. For example 'biscuit' – meaning twice baked.

Spoof sentences

Objective covered
W5 *The spellings of high-frequency words including common homophones.*

Aim
To collect, define and use a selection of homophones.

Resources
Dictionaries.

Activity
⊛ Write the following sentence on the board:

> The actors took there bough at the end of they're our long play.

⊛ Ask the students to write out the correct version:

> The actors took their bow at the end of their hour-long play.

Remind the students that all the spelling errors were examples of wrongly chosen homophones.

⊛ Now ask the students to make up similar sentences. They should then pass their sentences on to others who replace incorrect words with the appropriate homophone.

Differentiation
⊛ ⇓ Provide a bank of common homophones to play with, such as: 'to', 'two' and 'too'; 'hear' and 'here'.

Follow up
⊛ Students could make homophone dictionaries as an ongoing project and devise strategies for learning a specific set of homophones. These could be displayed in poster form.

Whose apostrophe is it anyway?

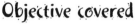

Objective covered

W6 *The use of the apostrophe including: omissions; the possessive apostrophe; apostrophising plurals, e.g. 'ladies' coats', and words ending in 's'; the exception of possessive pronouns.*

Aim

To revise and consolidate students' understanding of the use of the apostrophe to show possession.

Activity

⚙ Remind the students that the apostrophe is used to show that something belongs to a person or a thing. Choose an object belonging to someone in the class. Hold it up and say a sentence to describe it, for example 'Tom's pencil case is furry.'

⚙ Ask the class to tell you to whom the pencil case belongs. Take the answer and write it up on the board using the following formula: 'The pencil case is Tom's. It is Tom's pencil case.' Make the point that the apostrophe shows you the answer to the question, 'Who does it belong to?'

⚙ Ask the students to work in pairs. They should take turns in the call and response model that you have demonstrated.

⚙ Then, as a class, use the following list of nouns to be the possessors of an object.

Ruth	People	The ladies
The boy	Women	Marcus
The boys	Children	James

⚙ Remind the students to keep asking, 'Who does it belong to?' The apostrophe always goes after the final letter of the answer. You will also need to remind them that plural nouns drop the final 's'.

Mind the gap

Objective covered / aim

W6 *The use of the apostrophe, including omissions.*

Resources

Individual whiteboards and pens, or cards for each letter of the following words:

cannot	does not	we have	we are	do not
would not	I will	he will	he is	it is

Activity

✸ Either choose one word to be the focus for every team or assign a different word to each team. Arrange the students in teams. The size of each team will vary according to the total number of letters in each of the words or phrases used. For example, 'we have' forms a team of seven students – one student for each letter and one for an apostrophe.

✸ Each team should use the cards or individual whiteboards to write out the letters of the focus word and one apostrophe. When the words are prepared, separate the students with the apostrophes from the rest of the teams, placing the words at one end of the room and the apostrophes at the other.

✸ On a given signal, each team of letters must arrange themselves in a line to form the focus word(s). The apostrophes then move the necessary letters out of the way before inserting themselves into the correct position within the contracted word. The quickest team to form the correctly contracted word is the winner.

Differentiation

✸ ⇩ Only use phrases containing the same verb or the same negative so that a particular contracted letter string is reinforced, for example, 'I have', 'you have', 'they have', 'we have'.

Follow up

✸ Ask each team to formulate a rule for shortening words.

Active apostrophes

Objective covered

W6 *The use of the apostrophe including: omissions; the possessive apostrophe; apostrophising plurals, e.g. 'ladies' coats', and words ending in 's'; the exception of possessive pronouns.*

Aim

To revise and consolidate students' understanding of the apostrophe in contracting words and to draw attention to when we use contracted forms of words in speech and writing.

Resources

Small cards – one for each of the following words:

cannot, can't	influenza, 'flu
will not, won't	we are, we're
she will, she'll	it is, it's
we have, we've	had not, hadn't
does not, doesn't	they have, they've
would not, wouldn't	she had, she'd
they are, they're	he is, he's
because, 'cos	

Activity

⊛ Deal out the cards, one to each student.

⊛ Ask the students to move around the room to find their 'partner' card. When all students are paired up, ask each pair to improvise a conversation using both forms of the word.

For example, 'It's dark.' 'Yes, it is.'

Differentiation

⊛ ⇑ Find more words like 'flu which use apostrophes of contraction at their start.

Word webs

Objective covered
W7 *The spellings of key words in each subject.*

Aim
To revise word webs as a strategy for learning spelling and vocabulary.

Resources
Dictionaries.

Activity
⊛ Model this word web:

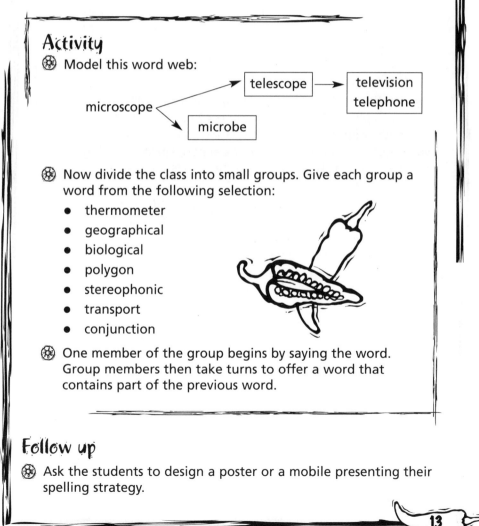

⊛ Now divide the class into small groups. Give each group a word from the following selection:
- thermometer
- geographical
- biological
- polygon
- stereophonic
- transport
- conjunction

⊛ One member of the group begins by saying the word. Group members then take turns to offer a word that contains part of the previous word.

Follow up
⊛ Ask the students to design a poster or a mobile presenting their spelling strategy.

I am an expert

Objective covered

W1d *Review, consolidate and secure the spelling conventions covered in Year 7 which include prefixes and suffixes.*

Aim

To teach the spelling convention for the suffix '-cian'.

Activity

- ✸ Write the suffix '-cian' on the board. Ask the students to write down any word that ends in this suffix. Give them the example 'physician' if you think they need it.
- ✸ Share the examples generated. Write some of them on the board.
- ✸ Ask the students if they can tell you what this suffix tells us. (It indicates that someone is an expert. The words made by adding this suffix are always nouns.)
- ✸ Ask the class if they can spot a pattern in the spelling of the root words to which the suffix '-cian' has been added. (All the root words end in the letters '-ic'.)
- ✸ Ask the students to invent a root word ending in '-ic' to which they can add the suffix '-cian' to create a new expert.
- ✸ Share the words made. You could ask the class to guess what some of the invented words mean.

Hint

- ✸ If the students struggle, tell them to think of words ending in '-ic', for example: 'statician' – an expert in static things; 'septician' – an expert in septic things; 'Arctician' – an expert in the Arctic; 'Atlantician' – an expert in the Atlantic.

Follow up

- ✸ Write these scrambled words on the board and ask the students to unscramble them.

  Sciimaun (musician) Opictalini (politician) Tact. Is it a sin? (statistician)

Apostrophe accuracy

Objective covered

W1e *Review, consolidate and secure the spelling conventions covered in Year 7 which include apostrophes.*

Aim

To enable students to revise correct use of the apostrophe for possession and omission.

Resources

Individual whiteboards and pens.

Activity

- Revise the use of possessive apostrophes, both plural and singular, for example:

  Jessica's mobile phone

  Students' mobile phones

- Divide the class into five groups. Write the following words on the board:

  dog   teacher   singer

- As in the above example, each group should write out two sentences for each word – one using the apostrophe for singular possession and one for plural, for example:

  The dog's ear was bitten off by the cat.

  The dogs' kennels were a long way from the house.

- Ask the students to share their sentences with the class.

Follow up

- Students could design a PowerPoint presentation entitled 'Apostrophe Accuracy!'

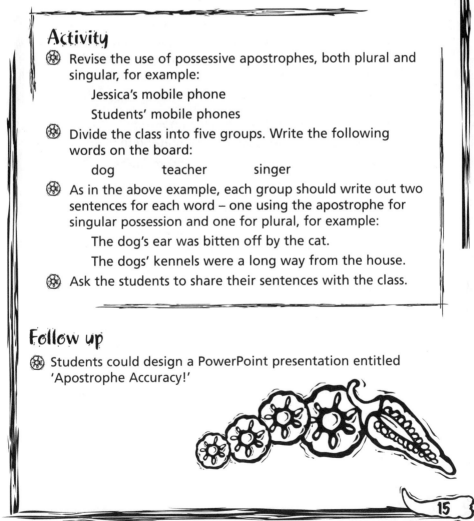

Sound snap

YEAR 8

Objective covered / aim
W1f *Review, consolidate and secure the spelling conventions covered in Year 7 which include homophones.*

Resources
Individuals whiteboards and pens.

Activity

⊛ Display a list of homophone words. Use the list below or focus on the key homophones your students seem to have trouble with. (Do not write the words in pairs unless the attainment of the class suggests this would be helpful.)

sure, shore	scene, seen	steak, stake
their, there	leak, leek	sight, site
to, too	wait, weight	fate, fete
know, no	here, hear	sum, some
great, grate	peace, piece	rode, road
board, bored	break, brake	

⊛ Ask each student to write one of the words on an individual whiteboard. Then swap the whiteboards around, face down so that nobody knows what is written.

⊛ Pick a student to define their word. For example, 'site' could be defined as the location of an activity or an object/thing.

⊛ Ask the class to spell the homophone partner to the word. In the case of 'site' they should spell out 'sight'.

⊛ Continue until all the words are revealed.

⊛ Ask the students to pair up with their homophone partner.

⊛ Ask them if there are any homophone pairs that could in fact be trios, for example: 'to', 'too', 'two'; 'their', 'there', 'they're'; 'rode', 'road', 'rowed'.

Red hot spelling tips

Objective covered

W2 *Spell accurately all high-frequency words and new terms from all subject areas.*

Aim

To encourage students to find their own techniques for remembering difficult spellings.

Resources

Individual whiteboards and pens.

Activity

- ✺ Ask the students to work in pairs of similar spelling ability.

- ✺ Each pair must think of two words that they have difficulty in spelling.

- ✺ Once they have chosen their two words, each pair of students has five minutes to design a simple teaching aid to memorise each word. For example, they could use a visual aid, mnemonic or written explanation of why the word is spelt as it is.

- ✺ These teaching aids can be shown on individual whiteboards, recorded in exercise books or used for a display. Alternatively, they could be collated to produce spelling resources for younger students.

Chronic phonics

Objective covered

W9 *Sound out words phonemically and by syllables.*

Aim

To investigate alternative representations of phonemes within words in an amusing way. (This should also develop understanding of some common spelling errors.)

Activity

⊛ Display the following on the board or OHP:

> Edewkayshun Rools!

> Taybulls faw sail.

⊛ Ask the students to identify what is wrong with the way the words are spelt. Point out that the speller has made guesses that are phonically perfect, but unfortunately English is not phonically consistent.

⊛ Now ask the students to try some 'chronic phonic' spellings of their own.

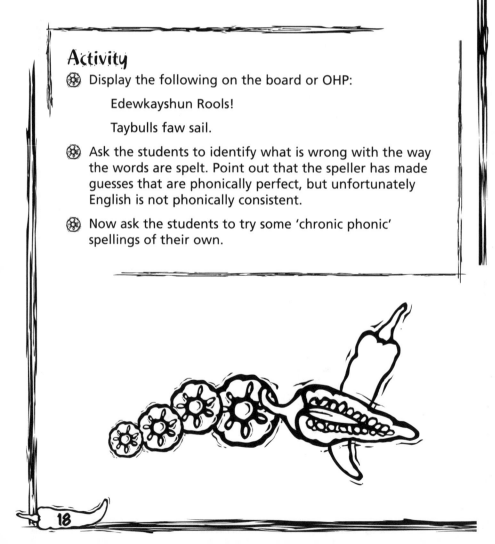

Every syllable counts

Objective covered
W9 *Sound out words phonemically and by syllables.*

Aim
To develop awareness of syllables within words.

Activity

⚙ Ask the students for ways of identifying the number of syllables in a word. Point out that the syllables in any word are built around the separate vowel sounds in it.

⚙ Ask the students to see how quickly they can count the syllables in given words. They should then try to solve these syllable puzzles:

- What is the most syllabic word you can think of?

- Write a sentence in which the first word has one syllable, the second has two and so on, for example:

    The daily newspaper recommended international autobiographies unenthusiastically.

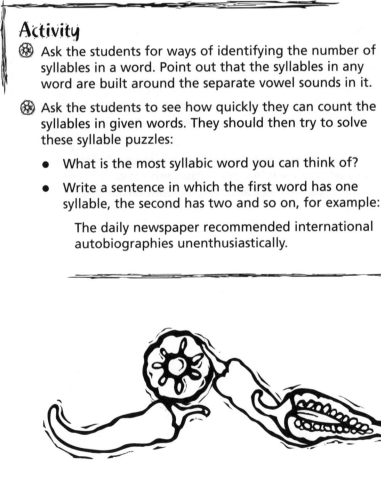

Sounding off

Objective covered

W6d *Devise their own ways to improve their spelling, building on strategies from Year 7 including sounding out and syllabifying.*

Aim

To secure an understanding that the syllables or beats in a word are built around a vowel sound and to use this knowledge as part of a range of spelling strategies.

Activity

⚽ Remind the students about syllables and point out that the syllables in any word are built around the separate vowel sounds it has. Use the following as examples.

- England: two syllables, two separate vowel sounds.
- Beach: one syllable, one vowel sound.

⚽ Now put the students into small teams. These can vary in size according to the attainment of the students. Their challenge is to see which team can come up with the longest list of football teams, each football team containing one more syllable than the last. For example: Leeds, Chelsea, Everton, Aston Villa, Nottingham Forest, Manchester United.

⚽ Share the lists generated. Can anybody get beyond a six-syllable team? (Wolverhampton Wanderers has seven.) Get the students to chant the names or clap them out so that the syllables are emphasised.

Follow up

⚽ Ask pairs of students to create a dialogue that begins with two syllables and then goes to three and so on. For example:

'Hello.'

'Hello, John.'

'Well, how are you?'

'Fine. How about you?'

'Oh, things could be better.'

Letter strings

Objective covered

W6e *Devise their own ways to improve their spelling, building on strategies from Year 7 including memorising critical features.*

Aim

To draw students' attention to difficult letter strings in order to memorise them.

Resources

Prepare a list of words using the letter strings you wish to concentrate on, for example:

- might, ought, thoughtfully, sight, weightless (ght)
- fetch, match, etch, itchy, scratchy, ratchet (tch)

Activity

- ✸ Explain what a mnemonic is and that you can use this strategy to memorise the tricky part of a word, not just the whole word. Suggest a mnemonic for the letter strings you've chosen, for example, 'giants hate tinies' or 'toads chew horses'.

- ✸ Ask the students to get into pairs. Each pair should devise their own mnemonics.

- ✸ Say that you are going to say some words that include the letter strings they have just memorised through the mnemonic. Give them some words from your prepared list and ask the students to write them down. Ask them to show the words they have written.

Follow up

- ✸ Choose a letter string and ask students to think of as many words as they can.

Word families

Objective covered / aim

W6f *Devise their own ways to improve their spelling, building on strategies from Year 7 including drawing on word structures, families and derivations.*

Resources

Dictionaries.

Activity

- ✾ Write 'port' on the board. Explain that this is a Latin root that means 'carry' and it is a part of many English words to do with carrying; for example 'porter', 'portable'.

- ✾ How many words containing the root 'port' can the students find? They can use dictionaries, if needed. Give a time limit of, say, four minutes.

- ✾ When the time is up, collect the students' lists of words and see who has found the most. Many will derive from the root (e.g. portal, transport, export). Some will be no relation (e.g. sport). Have the students found any words that they can clearly see are members of the 'port' family? Which words are they unsure about?

- ✾ Other roots that can be used for this activity:

Root	Comes from	Means
bio	Greek	life
cept	Latin	take
form	Latin	form, shape
graph	Greek	write
script	Latin	write
spect	Latin	look
phone	Greek	voice
hydr	Greek	water
fect	Latin	cause, make
vid/vis	Latin	see
cis	Latin	cut
cent	Latin	hundred

Tricky spellings

Objective covered

W6g *Devise their own ways to improve their spelling, building on strategies from Year 7 including using analogy.*

Aim

To show how the spelling of many long, unfamiliar and made-up words can be worked out through a combination of simple phonic knowledge and analogy.

Activity

❁ Read out one of the made-up words from the list below, for example 'splake'. Explain that phonics suggest that it could be spelt 'splaik' or even 'splayk', but English words rhyming with this all end in '-ake', for example 'take' or 'make'.

❁ Explain to the students that they are going to have a spelling test on made-up words. Use the words listed below.

splake	rainfully	telefaction
flice	fribulous	transdictional
blay	explification	dentrified
triffs	topifaction	ultimologist
dright (or drite)	extapulation	phonometer
fragged	hyperficial	polygraphic
scoping	intrafusion	audiophobia
clatches	aquaphonic	gyrotraction
rainful	premundation	laminography

Differentiation

❁ ⇑ Ask the students to make up their own words by analogy to other English words. These could then be used for further rounds of 'Tricky spellings' or for 'Call my bluff', page 33.

Wordology

YEAR 9

Objective covered / aim

W4b *Address personal difficulties with words through strategies which include applying knowledge of word origins, families and morphology.*

Activity

- ✸ Remind the students that a morpheme is the smallest unit of meaning in a word. For example 'signify' contains the morpheme 'sign', which means a mark or a token. It comes from the Latin word, signum.

- ✸ Ask the students to work in pairs. They should brainstorm any words they know that contain the morpheme 'sign'. Some examples are 'significant', 'signal', 'signature', 'signet', 'signatory' and 'signpost'.

- ✸ Ask how knowing the origin of the morpheme helps you to work out both the meanings and the spellings of the words students have listed.

- ✸ Give the students the morpheme '-logy'. Tell them this morpheme is a suffix and it means 'the study of', as in 'biology' – the study of life or living things. Tell the students that you are going to give them some made-up words that use this morpheme. Remind them that they know how to spell the morpheme and that they should think about the spelling of the other morphemes contained within the words you give them. Say that you want them to spell each word as you give it and also work out its meaning. Three examples are given below.

  - dictology: 'dict' coming from 'dictionary' and 'dictation'.

  - photology: 'photo' coming from 'photograph', 'photosynthesis' and 'telephoto'.

  - verdology: as in 'verdure', 'verdant', 'verdigris' and the French word 'vert'.

Differentiation

- ✸ ⇑ Students should make up their own '-ologies'.

It's all Greek to me

Objective covered
W10 *Draw on analogies to known words, roots, derivations, word families, morphology and familiar spelling patterns.*

Aim
To apply a variety of strategies in order to learn and remember spellings.

Resources
Individual whiteboards and pens.
Dictionaries.

Activity

⊛ Write examples of Greek word roots on the board:

    photo (light)   geo (earth)   graph (write)

⊛ Ask the students to work in pairs. Each pair should write three words on their whiteboards using the above roots.

⊛ Divide the class into five groups and give each group one of the following root words:

    tele   stereo   phobia   therm   auto

⊛ Each group should find two real words using a dictionary and invent a third. All three words should contain the given root. The rest of the class then try to guess which is the invented word.

Follow up

⊛ The students could use dictionaries to find roots other than the ones provided above. You could apply the above strategies to Latin root words, for example:

    dict (speak)

    sign (mark)

    spec (see)

Word pairs

Objective covered
W15 *Use a dictionary and a thesaurus with speed and skill.*

Aim
To use a thesaurus to find synonyms.

Resources
Thesauruses.
10 small cards per student (these can be made from scrap paper).

Activity

⊛ Ask each student to use a thesaurus to find five pairs of synonyms. One word in each pair should be fairly common, the synonym can be more obscure. For example, 'reward' and 'remuneration'. The students should write each word on a separate card.

⊛ Organise the class into groups of three or four. The cards from the students in the group should be shuffled and placed face down on the table. In turn, each student should turn over two cards. If the cards are a matching pair then the student should keep them; if not, the cards should be turned face down again. The student to collect the most pairs is the winner.

Dictionary speed challenge

Objective covered

W15 *Use a dictionary and a thesaurus with speed and skill.*

Aim

To improve speed and confidence when handling dictionaries.

Resources

Dictionaries.

Activity

⊛ Split the class into teams.

⊛ Call out a word.

⊛ The first student to locate the word in their dictionary earns a point for their team.

Hint

⊛ Ask successful players to define the skills and tips that assist speed with dictionaries and alphabetic texts.

Differentiation

⊛ ⇑ Call out words that are not listed as main header words, for example 'assumption', which is usually listed under 'assume'. This could prompt discussion of word families and morphology.

Get the joke?

Objective covered

W17 *Understand and have the terminology to describe the role of word classes, e.g. preposition, auxiliary verb.*

Activity

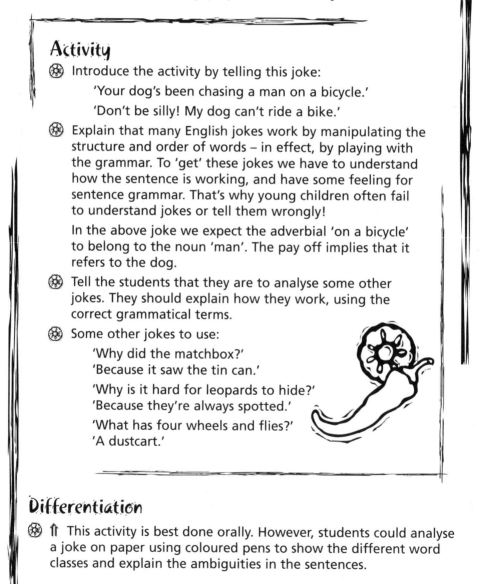

⊛ Introduce the activity by telling this joke:

'Your dog's been chasing a man on a bicycle.'

'Don't be silly! My dog can't ride a bike.'

⊛ Explain that many English jokes work by manipulating the structure and order of words – in effect, by playing with the grammar. To 'get' these jokes we have to understand how the sentence is working, and have some feeling for sentence grammar. That's why young children often fail to understand jokes or tell them wrongly!

In the above joke we expect the adverbial 'on a bicycle' to belong to the noun 'man'. The pay off implies that it refers to the dog.

⊛ Tell the students that they are to analyse some other jokes. They should explain how they work, using the correct grammatical terms.

⊛ Some other jokes to use:

'Why did the matchbox?'
'Because it saw the tin can.'

'Why is it hard for leopards to hide?'
'Because they're always spotted.'

'What has four wheels and flies?'
'A dustcart.'

Differentiation

⊛ ⇧ This activity is best done orally. However, students could analyse a joke on paper using coloured pens to show the different word classes and explain the ambiguities in the sentences.

Verbifying

Objective covered / aim

W19 Investigate and apply lexical patterns, e.g. adding '-ify' to an adjective to create a verb.

Resources

Individual whiteboards and pens.

Activity

❀ Explain that some adjectives can be turned into verbs or nouns by adding '-ify'. For example, 'solid' becomes 'solidify'. Ask the students what 'solidify' means. Write sentences on the board to illustrate word usage:

- If hot metal is left to cool, it will solidify.

- Hot metal solidifies when it is left to cool.

❀ As a class, play 'Guess the ending'. Call out a word from the list below. Tell students that they should add '-ify', '-ate', '-ise' or '-ity' to the word. They should show the result on their whiteboards (some words have more than one ending).

     stupid   liquid   real   formal   equal

Answers

stupidity	liquidate	realise	formalise	equalise
	liquidise	reality	formality	equality
	liquidity			

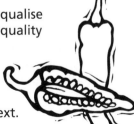

Differentiation

❀ ⇑ Ask the students to use the words in context.

Follow up

❀ Investigate more suffixes, for example '-ly' when added to an adjective.

Connectives, connectives...

Objective covered

W20 *Expand the range of link words and phrases used to signpost texts, including links of time (then, later, meanwhile) and cause (so, because, since).*

Aim

To expand repertoire of words and phrases to link sentences. To develop understanding of how these connectives affect the cohesion of a text.

Activity

❋ Display the following or prepare a set of cards, one for each connective.

Once upon a time	Despite this
Just then	Afterwards
Fortunately	Moreover
Unfortunately	Nevertheless
However	On the other hand
For this reason	Also
Later	Anyway
Meanwhile	After all
Therefore	As a result of this
Consequently	At that moment

❋ Tell the students that they are going to create a group story. In turn, each student should tell one line of the story. Each sentence has to begin with a connective from the list.

Differentiation

❋ ⇑ Ask the students to sort the cards according to the different jobs done by the connectives. For example: to add to; to contradict; to explain cause and effect; to indicate time.

Continental connections

Objective covered / aim

W22 *Draw links between words in different languages, e.g. Haus – house; femme – feminine.*

Resources

Individual whiteboards and pens.

Activity

✸ Divide the class into teams. Reveal the following list of German words one at a time. Ask the students to work out what they mean in English and display their answers on whiteboards. Award one point for each correct answer. Discuss the similarities and differences between the words.

Familie (family)	Tisch (table)	Brot (bread)
Geburtstag (birthday)	rot (red)	blau (blue)
Schule (school)	Pullover (pullover)	Socken (socks)
hallo (hello)	Apfel (apple)	Hund (dog)

✸ Play a game of 'True or false?' Students must indicate whether each word is a correct French word.

chocolate (F – chocolat)	histori (F – histoire)
blue (F – bleu)	famille (T)
nom (T)	la danse (T)
adorer (T)	vocabulary (F – vocabulaire)

Follow up

✸ Ask the students to compile a list that shows how other languages have coined English words, for example 'skateboard', 'weekend', 'chewing gum', 'T-shirt', 'Internet', 'e-mail', 'cool'.

✸ Ask the students to find examples of English words that have been 'borrowed' from other languages.

Say what it means

Objective covered

W7c *Review and develop their ability to understand and explain exactly what words mean in particular contexts.*

Aim

To define important words within strict limits.

Activity

⊛ Ask the students to work in pairs. They should define the word 'glove' in six or seven words. They should then try to define it in two or three words. Hear some of the definitions and discuss problems and strategies.

⊛ Repeat the process with other words. At first restrict the words to concrete nouns; for example 'bucket', 'parrot', 'potato', 'armchair'.

⊛ Other types of word that could be used for this activity are:

- Abstract nouns (e.g. silence, music, pride, truth). These are much harder than concrete nouns.

- Other word classes (e.g. adjectives: angry, perfect, comfortable, magnificent).

- Thematic words (usually abstract nouns) referring to themes or issues raised by a text studied in English lessons (e.g. *Macbeth*: ambition, guilt, conscience, supernatural).

- Keywords from other subject areas (e.g. history: government, revolution, bias; geography: climate, pollution, environment, population, settlement; science: reaction, nutrient, mass).

- Words that have different meanings in different contexts (e.g. table: furniture, maths, geography; volume: music, maths, books; frame: building, snooker, art; scale: music, maths, fish). Specify the context in which you want a definition.

Call my bluff

Objective covered / aim

W9 *Appreciate the precise meaning of specialist vocabulary for each school subject, and use specialist terms aptly in their own writing.*

Resources

Dictionaries.
Individual whiteboards and pens.

Activity

⊛ Remind the students how to play *Call my bluff* by setting up a quick game as a class. Give three students slips of paper on which are written one true and two false definitions of the word 'prototype', for example:

- Prototype is the latest model of sports car from Jaguar.
- Before a product is manufactured commercially, a first unit is produced and tested so that it can be changed and improved. This is called a prototype.
- Prototype is a portable computer keyboard.

Ask them to read out their definitions for the rest of the class to vote for the one that they believe to be correct.

⊛ Divide the class into teams. Give each team a complex subject-specific word, for example:

polyhedra	pentatonic	revolution
expressionist	congruent	

⊛ Next, ask the students to check the meaning of the word in the dictionary and write the definition on their whiteboards. Then they need to think of one more definition that is not true. When students have finished, they take turns to present their true and false definition for the rest of the class to choose between.

Hint

⊛ Encourage the students to be creative and make their classmates think by identifying possible links with other words, for example, polyhedra: 'A jellyfish native to the Polynesian Islands'.

Yes, but...

Objective covered / aim

W10 *Extend the range of prepositions and connectives used to express reservations.*

Activity

- ⊛ Tell the students that you are going to ask them to use connectives that express reservation to create sentences of excuses. The aim of the game is to find a polite way of getting out of an invitation.

- ⊛ Model the following:

    'Can you play for the rugby team tonight?'
    'I'd love to but I've got wash my hair.'

- ⊛ Ask the students to work in pairs. They should create their own two-sentence conversation containing an invitation and a polite refusal. Share some of their examples.

- ⊛ Now introduce the following list of connectives to express reservation:

    although   if   while/whilst   unless   even though

- ⊛ Model a refusal starting with one of these connectives, for example:

    'Can you play for the rugby team tonight?'
    'Although I'd love to play, I've got to wash my hair.'

- ⊛ Now ask the students to create other two-sentence conversations, each excuse beginning with one of the connectives given.

Hint

- ⊛ Point out that it is the convention to place a comma after the subordinate clause when it opens the sentence.

Follow up

- ⊛ Use this starter as a basis for a piece of drama or writing dialogue/script.

How do you say that?

Objective covered/aim

W13 *Understand the implications when a word is in quotation marks or used ironically.*

Activity

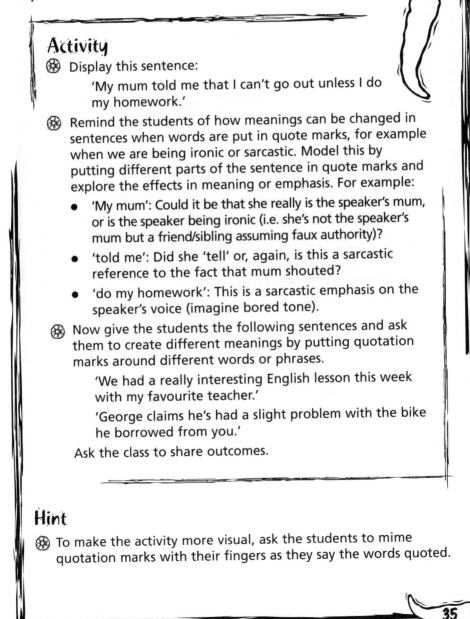

- Display this sentence:

    'My mum told me that I can't go out unless I do my homework.'

- Remind the students of how meanings can be changed in sentences when words are put in quote marks, for example when we are being ironic or sarcastic. Model this by putting different parts of the sentence in quote marks and explore the effects in meaning or emphasis. For example:

    - 'My mum': Could it be that she really is the speaker's mum, or is the speaker being ironic (i.e. she's not the speaker's mum but a friend/sibling assuming faux authority)?

    - 'told me': Did she 'tell' or, again, is this a sarcastic reference to the fact that mum shouted?

    - 'do my homework': This is a sarcastic emphasis on the speaker's voice (imagine bored tone).

- Now give the students the following sentences and ask them to create different meanings by putting quotation marks around different words or phrases.

    'We had a really interesting English lesson this week with my favourite teacher.'

    'George claims he's had a slight problem with the bike he borrowed from you.'

    Ask the class to share outcomes.

Hint

- To make the activity more visual, ask the students to mime quotation marks with their fingers as they say the words quoted.

Hi tech

Objective covered

W14 *Collect and comment on examples of language change, e.g. new words associated with electronic communication and ICT.*

Aim

To compile and discuss words and phrases associated with ICT and to reinforce students' understanding through a speaking and listening activity.

Resources

Dictionaries.

Activity

- ⊛ Brainstorm as many words as possible to do with ICT. Focus on the word 'web' and ask the students to look the word up in the dictionary. (Any structure or fabric formed by weaving and interweaving.) Ask them why they think a 'web page' and 'World Wide Web' are thus called. Take feedback and comment on examples.

- ⊛ Start a list of words/phrases of ICT-related vocabulary, for example:

spam	hacker	e-mail	server
virus	hard drive	sound/video card	
crash	cookies	motherboard	

- ⊛ Get the students to add to the list. Ask them to discuss what the terms mean. Using dictionaries can they work out why each particular word has evolved?

- ⊛ Ask the students to get into pairs. They should take turns explaining each term as though talking to someone who knows nothing about ICT.

Follow up

- ⊛ Students could compile their own ICT dictionaries, for younger students, incorporating the words above and others collected through personal research.

What do you mean?

Objective covered

W7 *Recognise layers of meaning in the writer's choice of words.*

Aim

To explore how implicit meanings are conveyed, by changing the verb of speech.

Activity

❋ Write the following sentence on the board:

> 'You could be a rocket scientist, Dave,' laughed Barney.

Ask the students to identify what is implied by 'laughed'. (That David is stupid.)

❋ Ask the students to get into pairs. Each pair should change the verb of speech in order to change the implied meaning. They could use 'suggested', 'exclaimed', 'advised' or 'asked' in place of 'laughed'. The pairs should then share their sentences with the class.

❋ Give the sentence:

> 'Come here, Shenaz,' said Karen.

Still in pairs, the students should change the verb of speech so that the implied meaning is modified.

❋ Finally, write this sentence on the board:

> 'Come here, Shenaz,' whispered Karen wearily.

Ask the students to change the adverb (wearily) as well as the verb of speech (whispered).

Follow up

❋ Experiment with adverbial phrases.

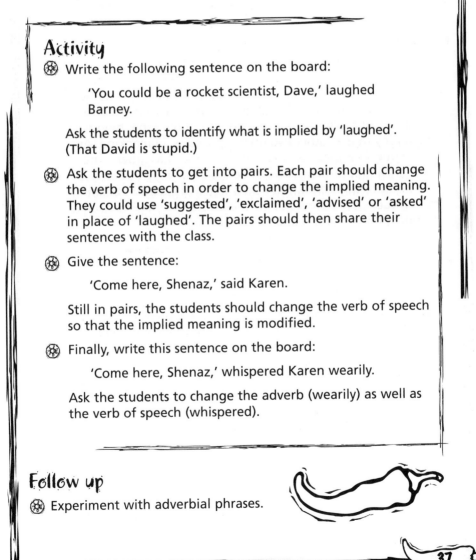

Joined up thinking 1

Objective covered

W8 *Recognise how lines of thought are developed and signposted through the use of connectives, e.g. nonetheless, consequently, furthermore.*

Aim

To identify the key words and phrases that signal the development of an idea or an argument in a piece of text.

Resources

Sample text on the board, OHT or as paper copies:

> The rhinoceros is a large mammal with a remarkably tough hide and an equally fierce horn on its nose. Consequently it has few natural predators. Until the latter part of the twentieth century it was one of evolution's success stories but now the rhino has fallen prey to that other evolutionary success, humankind. As competition for space on the plains of Africa has grown, the natural habitat of the rhino has been increasingly threatened. The result of this, combined with a somewhat bizarre belief in the efficacious properties of powdered rhino horn, has been an alarming fall in rhino numbers.

Activity

- ⊛ Show the class the sample text.
- ⊛ The students should work in pairs. Ask them to identify the words and phrases that develop the line of thinking in the text. Ask the students, where possible, to identify the links within a single sentence. For example 'until … but now', 'as … increasingly'. Also ask them to sum up the paragraph in one sentence. Share outcomes.
- ⊛ Say that in the next lesson the class will be asked to create their own paragraph of text using connectives to develop the line of thinking.

Joined up thinking 2

Objective covered

W8 *Recognise how lines of thought are developed and signposted through the use of connectives, e.g. nonetheless, consequently, furthermore.*

Aim

To use key words and phrases to signal the development of an idea or an argument in a piece of text.

Activity

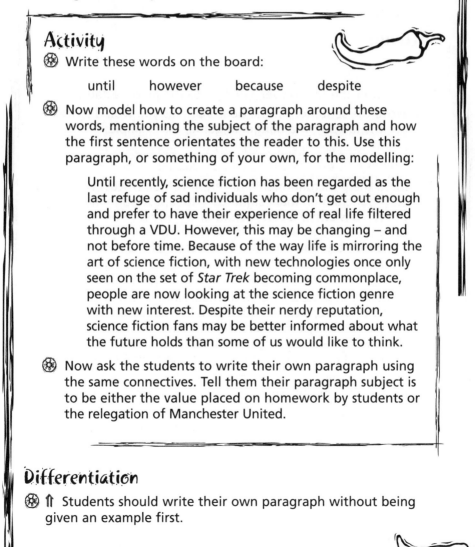

⊛ Write these words on the board:

    until   however   because   despite

⊛ Now model how to create a paragraph around these words, mentioning the subject of the paragraph and how the first sentence orientates the reader to this. Use this paragraph, or something of your own, for the modelling:

> Until recently, science fiction has been regarded as the last refuge of sad individuals who don't get out enough and prefer to have their experience of real life filtered through a VDU. However, this may be changing – and not before time. Because of the way life is mirroring the art of science fiction, with new technologies once only seen on the set of *Star Trek* becoming commonplace, people are now looking at the science fiction genre with new interest. Despite their nerdy reputation, science fiction fans may be better informed about what the future holds than some of us would like to think.

⊛ Now ask the students to write their own paragraph using the same connectives. Tell them their paragraph subject is to be either the value placed on homework by students or the relegation of Manchester United.

Differentiation

⊛ ⇑ Students should write their own paragraph without being given an example first.

Sentence detectives

Objective covered

Sn1a *Recognising and using subordinate clauses.*

Aim

To recognise and explore patterns of written language use. Consolidate understanding of punctuation usage to mark clause boundaries and so on.

Activity

⊛ Make up a sentence but do not share it with the class, for example:

> After the film is over, we'll go to the pizza restaurant.

⊛ Write the sentence on the board/OHP as you would write out the letters for a hangman game, for example:

_ _ _ _ _ / _ _ _ / _ _ _ _ / _ _ / _ _ _ _ , / _ _ ' _ _ /
_ _ / _ _ / _ _ _ / _ _ _ _ _ / _ _ _ _ _ _ _ _ _ _ .

Mark the punctuation in a different colour. Discuss what each punctuation mark signifies. (The apostrophe means the word is either a contraction or a possessive noun. The comma is used as a boundary between a main clause and a subordinate clause placed at the start of the sentence.)

⊛ Use a scoring system. For example, the class have a bank of ten points and buy letters at a cost of three points each. Students can guess a letter or a whole word: a wrong guess loses two points; a correct guess wins two points. Alternatively use the simpler system where the class have three lives and lose one for each wrong guess. Students can guess the whole sentence at any point but an incorrect guess loses the game.

⊛ Play the game, adding letters or words as they are guessed or bought. The idea is to complete the sentence correctly before all the points are used up.

⊛ Give the students opportunities to discuss and justify their choices.

Drop that clause

Objective covered

Sn1 *Extend their use and control of complex sentences by:
recognising and using subordinate clauses; exploring the functions
of subordinate clauses; deploying subordinate clauses in a variety
of positions within the sentence.*

Aim

To practise creating subordinate clauses
beginning with which, who or whose.

Activity

⊛ Remind the students that a complex sentence contains a
main clause (big idea) and at least one subordinate clause
(supporting idea).

⊛ Identify the main and subordinate clauses in these sentences:

The dog, whose teeth were extremely large, growled
at me.

The roller blades, which I bought, go really fast.

My teacher, who is really strict, sets us homework every day.

⊛ Generate a list of subordinate clauses beginning with who,
whose or which, for example 'who liked to eat doughnuts'.

⊛ The students then choose a subordinate clause from the list
(or make up another) and write it down.

⊛ The students should swap their clauses with a partner.
They now have to drop their partner's clause into a
sentence. For example 'The dog, who liked to eat
doughnuts, needed to visit the dentist.'

Hint

⊛ Dropping subordinate clauses into a main clause can be
demonstrated through a range of media. For example: OHTs with
the clauses cut up; PowerPoint; interactive whiteboards.

What's the big idea?

Objective covered/aim

Sn1 *Extend their use and control of complex sentences by: recognising and using subordinate clauses; exploring the functions of subordinate clauses; deploying subordinate clauses in a variety of positions within the sentence.*

Resources

Individual whiteboards and pens.

Activity

⚙ Remind the students that the main clause contains the main idea and makes complete sense by itself.
A subordinate clause depends on the main clause for its full meaning and gives the reader more information about the action or the subject of the main clause.

⚙ Put this example on the board or OHP and identify the main and subordinate clauses as shown:

Sam didn't do his homework because he had left his books at school.

Main clause	Subordinate clause

⚙ Now write these sentences on the board or an OHT:

1   After she had kicked the cat, Becky felt much better.
2   Henry enjoyed the party although he had to leave before the end.
3   I won't watch the TV until I've finished the washing up.

⚙ Ask the students to identify the main and subordinate clauses in each example using individual whiteboards.

Answers

1 subordinate, main   2 main, subordinate   3 main, subordinate

Follow up

⚙ Provide a main/subordinate clause and ask the students to create a subordinate/main clause to go with it.

Move that clause

Objective covered / aim

Sn1 *Extend their use and control of complex sentences by: recognising and using subordinate clauses; exploring the functions of subordinate clauses; deploying subordinate clauses in a variety of positions within a sentence.*

Resources

Individual whiteboards and pens.

Activity

- Write the following on three individual whiteboards:
  - Becky and Simon
  - staggering under the weight of their shopping
  - caught the train home

- Ask for three volunteers and give one board to each. Ask them to arrange themselves so that the words form a complete sentence. Read it aloud. Ask the class if it is possible to arrange the words in any other way. Get volunteers to do this.

- Ask the students to get into groups of three. They should work out all the possible combinations for this example:
  - Ron
  - flopped into bed
  - tired from a day of Quidditch

- Draw attention to the use of non-finite verbs in the two worked examples (staggering and tired). Tell the students that the next sentences they construct for themselves are going to use this pattern.

- Still in groups of three, ask the students to create the following on their whiteboards: a main clause but with the name of the subject written separately on another whiteboard, a subordinate clause beginning with an '-ing' or an '-ed' verb. How many ways can the sentence be arranged?

Noun doodling

Objective covered
Sn2 *Expand nouns and noun phrases, e.g. by using a prepositional phrase.*

Aim
To explore pre- and post-modification of nouns as ways of adding interest and detail to writing.

Resources
Individual whiteboards and pens.

Activity
⊛ Explain that detail can be added to a single noun by adding other words like adjectives in front of the noun and by adding phrases beginning with a preposition after the noun. Write these examples on the board:

> road
> busy road
> alarmingly busy road
> the alarmingly busy road
> the alarmingly busy road near the children's playground

⊛ Tell the students that they are going to 'doodle with nouns' by creating little bits of description like the noun phrases on the board. Working in pairs, they should use the following nouns:

> cat　　penguin　　dream　　cake

⊛ Ask several pairs to display their work, using individual whiteboards, to the rest of the class.

Differentiation
⊛ ⇑ Ask the class to brainstorm how they would explain to somebody else what noun phrases do in writing.

⊛ ⇓ Only use pre-modification or only use post-modification.

Follow up
⊛ Students should find a recent piece of their own writing and decide on one example where the writing would be improved by expanding a noun into a noun phrase.

Whodunnit

Objective covered/aim

Sn5 *Use the active or the passive voice to suit purpose.*

Resources

The following (or similar) scenarios on card, an OHT or whiteboard:

- You've crashed the car.
- You've eaten the cake your mum made for tea.
- You've broken the video player.
- Your hamster has chewed a hole in the carpet.

Activity

- Remind the students that the passive voice doesn't reveal the agent of an action, for example: 'The cat was bitten.' Contrast this with the active voice: 'The fleas bit the cat.' Here, the agents of the action are revealed – they were the fleas.

- Model the following with a volunteer student:

  > Last night when I was at home I spilt hot chocolate on the living room carpet. I didn't want to own up to my friend/wife/husband/mother, so when I mentioned the stain I didn't say, 'I spilt hot chocolate on the carpet, sorry.' I said, 'It looks like hot chocolate has been spilt on the carpet.'

- Ask the students to get into pairs. They should now role-play 30-second dialogues that use the passive voice to avoid confessing who was the agent of the action in the chosen scenario.

- Share scenes and summarise what the passive voice is doing.

Secret agents

Objective covered

Sn5 *Use the active or the passive voice to suit purpose.*

Aim

To understand that the passive voice hides the agent
of the action in a sentence.

Activity

⊛ Display the following sentences:

> The artichoke was boiled by Catherine.
> The dinosaur was eaten by Farouk.
> The garage was haunted by Irene.

⊛ Point out the sentence structure and the alphabetical
sequence used. Ask the students to get into pairs. They
should think up the next two lines using the same
structure and sequence. Take examples and add the best
to your own lines on the board. Try and complete the
pattern, using up all the letters of the alphabet.

⊛ Point out that you have created a series of sentences that
use the passive voice. This means that the sentences
mention the recipient of the action – who the action was
done to – before giving away who did the action – the
agent of the action.

⊛ Rub out all the words after the verb in each sentence:

> The artichoke was boiled.
> The dinosaur was eaten.
> The garage was haunted.

⊛ Ask if each sentence still makes sense. Point out that the
agent of the action is now entirely hidden from the
reader.

⊛ Ask the students to write a sentence of their own which
hides the agent of the action.

Read all about it

Objective covered
Sn6 *Recognise and remedy ambiguity in sentences,*
e.g. unclear use of pronouns.

Aim
To raise awareness of the need to avoid ambiguous use
of pronouns and adverbials in writing.

Activity

- Display some of these headlines, adverts and news stories
  which are all reputed to have been published:
  - ENRAGED COW INJURES FARMER WITH AXE
  - STOLEN PAINTING FOUND BY TREE
  - JUDGE TO RULE ON NUDE BEACH
  - MAN STRUCK BY LIGHTNING FACES BATTERY CHARGE
  - SCHOOL DROPOUTS CUT IN HALF
  - DOG FOR SALE: eats anything, fond of children. (Small ad)
  - DON'T LET WORRY KILL YOU: LET THE CHURCH HELP
    (Church notice)
  - Ladies are requested not to have children at the bar.
    (Sign in Norwegian hotel)
  - Tired of cleaning yourself – let me do it. (Small ad)
  - A fifteen-year-old Croydon boy has been suspended by
    his head since last September because of his long hair.
    (*Times Educational Supplement*)

- Investigate the ambiguities – some are down to double
  meanings (e.g. 'battery charge'). Often the ambiguity
  stems from the use of an adverbial (e.g. 'with axe' in
  ENRAGED COW INJURES FARMER WITH AXE). The last
  three items include confusion over the pronouns and their
  references.

- Ask the students to invent new adverts, notices or headlines
  containing ambiguities. There are many websites that
  specialise in these, for example, the Vancouver English
  Centre website: www.english-usa.net/humor-jokes

Human speech marks

Objective covered

Sn7 *Use speech punctuation accurately to integrate speech into larger sentences.*

Aim

To explore correct punctuation of speech interactively.

Activity

- Write the following sentence on the board:

    The teacher said, 'I will be back soon.'

    Ask the class to point out the key punctuation features of the sentence.

- Give some students a 'punctuation role' to play in an extract of direct speech (speech marks, comma, capital letter, final punctuation mark). Read out the following sentence:

    'Would you like to come in?' asked the head teacher.

- Tell the students to stand at the front of the class in the order in which their designated punctuation occurs.

- In order to progress further, explore punctuation in the following sentence:

    'I will be back soon,' said the teacher, 'so make sure you work quietly.'

    Focus on the split sentence structure.

- In groups, the students make up examples of their own and take it in turns to be human punctuation. They should start with simple sentences first.

Move ing clauses

Objective covered/aim

Sn1 Combine clauses into complex sentences, using the comma effectively as a boundary signpost and checking for fluency and clarity, e.g. using non-finite clauses.

Activity

- Remind the students that a non-finite clause is built around a verb. The verb ends in '-ing' or '-ed'. When moved around a sentence, a non-finite clause does different things. Write these examples on the board:

   Katy, <u>who was sighing to herself</u>, began to do her homework. (Relative clause)

   Katy, <u>sighing to herself</u>, began to do her homework. (Relative clause which modifies the noun – Katy)

   <u>Sighing to herself</u>, Katy began to do her homework. (The clause is adverbial – it tells you about how Katy did it, thus modifying the verb.)

- Divide the class into groups. Ask them to create a sentence containing a non-finite clause. Give the students the following core sentences to play with:

   Paul played his drums.
   Jacinta danced the night away.
   Suna watched the football match.

- Students should feed back their sentences to the rest of the class. The class then identify where the non-finite clause is and what it is doing.

Follow up

- This starter lends itself to narrative writing activities where creativity, variation and clarity are called for.

Human sentences

Objective covered/aim

Sn1 *Combine clauses into complex sentences, using the comma effectively as a boundary signpost.*

Resources

Individual whiteboards and pens.

Activity

- Split the class into three groups: A, B and C.
- Everyone in groups A and B should write a clause, with no punctuation or capital letter, on their whiteboard (e.g. 'I felt ill' or 'a parrot flew past'). Ask them to check that the verb is in the past tense.
- Give everyone in group C a different subordinating connective to write on their board ('although', 'whenever', 'when', 'if', 'while', 'because', 'until', 'whereas', 'as', 'before', 'after').
- Now ask all the students to stand up with their boards. Group C students should take their pens with them.
- The students should form trios with one member from each of groups A to C to form a sentence with two clauses joined by a connective. The group C connective should be in the middle.
- Ask the trios to show their whiteboards so that everyone can see all the sentences made. Would it be better if some swaps were made?
- Next, the holder of the pen in each group should put in the capital letter and the full stop (e.g. 'I felt ill whenever a parrot flew past.').
- Now ask the trios to form a sentence beginning with the group C connective and then write in the appropriate punctuation (e.g. 'Whenever a parrot flew past, I felt ill.'). Note the comma separating the two clauses.

Act it out

Objective covered

Sn1 *Combine clauses into complex sentences, using the comma effectively as a boundary signpost and checking for fluency and clarity.*

Aim

To combine two simple sentences into one complex sentence, using a comma to signal the boundary between the main clause and the subordinate clause where necessary.

Activity

⊛ Display the following subordinate clauses:

- As she brushed her hair
- While he ate his cornflakes
- Having opened the door
- Looking carefully at what was written on the board

⊛ Tell the students that they need to think of a main clause to complete the sentence. Then tell them to create a short mime to illustrate their sentence. When the mimes are ready, ask some students to act out their mimes. The rest of the class should guess what the completed sentence is.

Differentiation

⊛ ⇓ Give the students sentences to mime, and ask them to identify the main clause in each one. For example;

- Cutting the bread carefully, Emma made a sandwich.
- Yawning sleepily, Parveen closed her book and rested her head on the table.
- Having cut down the tree, Jack wiped his hands on his shirt and headed for home.
- Once she had brought in the milk, Sara sat down to enjoy her favourite cereal.

The long and the short of it

Objective covered

Sn2 *Explore the impact of a variety of sentence structures, e.g. recognising when it is effective to use short direct sentences.*

Aim

To change one long sentence into a number of shorter sentences to create impact.

Activity

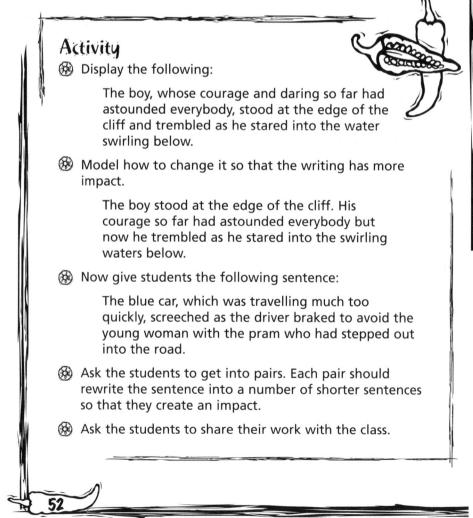

* Display the following:

> The boy, whose courage and daring so far had astounded everybody, stood at the edge of the cliff and trembled as he stared into the water swirling below.

* Model how to change it so that the writing has more impact.

> The boy stood at the edge of the cliff. His courage so far had astounded everybody but now he trembled as he stared into the swirling waters below.

* Now give students the following sentence:

> The blue car, which was travelling much too quickly, screeched as the driver braked to avoid the young woman with the pram who had stepped out into the road.

* Ask the students to get into pairs. Each pair should rewrite the sentence into a number of shorter sentences so that they create an impact.

* Ask the students to share their work with the class.

Mix and match 1

Objective covered
Sn3 *To make good use of the full range of punctuation, including colons and semi-colons.*

Aim
To teach students the correct use of colons (for introducing a list) and semi-colons (for separating long phrases in a list).

Activity

⊛ Remind the students of the function of colons and semi-colons in a sentence. Colons are written before a list or a quotation. One of the uses of the semi-colon is to separate long phrases in a list. Write the following example on the board.

> Here are some examples of cockney rhyming slang: apples and pears; plates of meat; bees and honey; whistle and flute.

⊛ Divide the class into groups. Give each group the start of a sentence which one student in each group writes on their whiteboard.

- The things I like about where I live are:
- If I could change the rules in my family they would be:
- The advantages of going to see a live concert are:
- My favourite holiday would include the following things:
- An ideal Saturday would be spent:

⊛ Other members of the group write one phrase in a list that completes the sentence, for example:

> My favourite holiday would include the following things: sea and sand; hot weather; good restaurants; a big swimming pool; a quiet hotel.

Give five minutes for this activity.

⊛ Ask the students to hold up their whiteboards in the order in which their phrase comes in the sentence.

Mix and match 2

Objective covered

Sn3 *To make good use of the full range of punctuation, including colons and semi-colons.*

Aim

To understand the function of a semi-colon when it is used instead of a connective to join together two clauses with related meanings.

Activity

※ Explain how the semi-colon can be used instead of a connective to link the ideas in two separate clauses together or instead of writing the clauses as two separate sentences. Explain that the semi-colon is used in this way when the meaning of the clauses is closely related, for example:

> It was raining heavily; Steve didn't go out into the garden as he usually did.

※ Explain that there are two main clauses here: 'It was raining' and 'Steve didn't go out into the garden as he usually did'. Emphasise that a link is implied between these two clauses.

※ Give this example and ask the students to identify the two separate clauses and the link that can be implied between them:

> I loved the film *Lord of the Rings*; the special effects were fantastic.

※ Ask the students to work in pairs. Give each pair one of the following clauses:

- The lesson was boring.
- The road was long and winding.

They should think of another clause that could be linked to the one given by using a semi-colon, for example:

> The lesson was boring; Ms Philips wasn't the most inspiring teacher of nuclear physics.

A tense affair

Objective covered

Sn4 *Explore the effects of changes in tense, e.g. past to present for vividness.*

Aim

To investigate the use of past or present tense in recounts.

Activity

- Display these three quotes:
    1. Hale knew, before they had been in Brighton three hours, that they meant to murder him.
    2. Some people are on the pitch. They think it's all over. It is now.
    3. A man walks into a pub with a parrot on his shoulder.

- Ask the students to work out the type of text in each case. (1 The first line of a novel – *Brighton Rock* by Graham Greene. 2 A famous football commentary. 3 The beginning of a joke.)

- Ask the students what they notice about the tense of the verb in each case.

- Can the students think why the speaker/writer of a joke (e.g. quote 3) might use the present tense? (The present tense brings immediacy to a recount, which makes it seem closer to the reader or listener.)

- Instruct the students to create three further quotes:
    - the first line of a piece of fiction
    - a line from a commentary of a live event
    - the first line of a joke.

- Ask the students to try changing the tense in their quotes. Does it alter the effect?

Follow up

- This activity can be followed up by collecting first sentences from fiction. Tell the students to sort them according to whether or not they are narrated in the past or the present tense.

What's the chance of that?

Objective covered

Sn5 *Recognise and exploit the use of conditionals and modal verbs when speculating, hypothesising or discussing possibilities.*

Aim

To investigate the way modal verbs are used to make judgements about the likelihood of events.

Activity

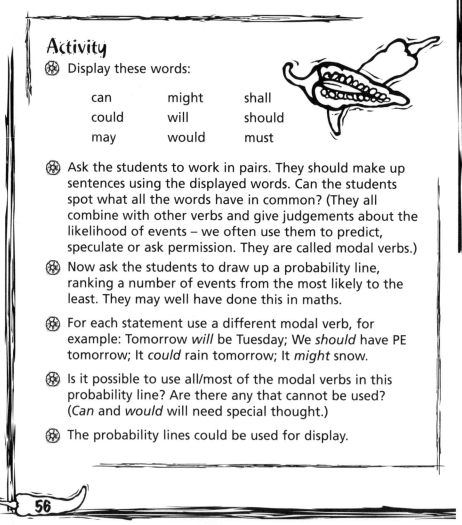

⊛ Display these words:

can	might	shall
could	will	should
may	would	must

⊛ Ask the students to work in pairs. They should make up sentences using the displayed words. Can the students spot what all the words have in common? (They all combine with other verbs and give judgements about the likelihood of events – we often use them to predict, speculate or ask permission. They are called modal verbs.)

⊛ Now ask the students to draw up a probability line, ranking a number of events from the most likely to the least. They may well have done this in maths.

⊛ For each statement use a different modal verb, for example: Tomorrow *will* be Tuesday; We *should* have PE tomorrow; It *could* rain tomorrow; It *might* snow.

⊛ Is it possible to use all/most of the modal verbs in this probability line? Are there any that cannot be used? (*Can* and *would* will need special thought.)

⊛ The probability lines could be used for display.

Complex combinations

Objective covered

Sn1 *Review and develop the meaning, clarity, organisation and impact of complex sentences in their own writing.*

Activity

⚙ Display these words:

> whenever
>
> shoes
>
> uproar

⚙ Ask the students to combine the three words into a sentence beginning with the first word (e.g. *Whenever* Sarah wore her red *shoes*, she caused an *uproar*). Can they create sentences that are meaningful, interesting or funny?

⚙ Demonstrate how the first word is the sort of conjunction that begins a subordinate clause. This means that the sentence will be complex, with a comma marking off the subordinate clause.

⚙ Take suggestions for words from students in further rounds of the game. In each case the first word(s) should be subordinating connectives, for example: 'although', 'because', 'when', 'if', 'whereas', 'owing to', 'despite', 'as a result of', 'some time after', 'thanks to', 'even though'. The next two words should be nouns. To make the game more difficult, these could be abstract nouns, for example: 'difference', 'harmony', 'peace', 'irritation'.

Differentiation

⚙ ⇑ For more confident writers, introduce other constraints on the sentence, for instance: in fewer than eight words; more than fifteen words; in the style of a weather forecast; in the style of a romantic letter; as an advertising slogan.

Smooth operator

Objective covered

Sn4 *Integrate speech, reference and quotation effectively into what they write.*

Aim

To develop students' skills in integrating quotations in their writing with a view to preparing them for the SATs Shakespeare paper.

Resources

Copies of a Shakespeare play the class are studying. Individual whiteboards and pens.

Activity

- Ask the students to find one quotation that reveals an important aspect of a main character in the Shakespeare play the group are studying. Model an example of integrating quotations, for example, for *Macbeth* Act 3, Scene 4:

  > After Macbeth sees Banquo's ghost he realises that there is no turning back and he must go to see the Witches to find out his future. He says to Lady Macbeth:
  >
  > > 'I am in blood
  > > Stepped in so far that should I wade no more,
  > > Returning were as tedious as go o'er.'
  >
  > Here, we see that Macbeth feels that it would be too much trouble to undo his terrible deeds, so he must continue. The use of the word 'blood' suggests that he still has murder on his mind.

- Point out the PEE pattern: **P**oint, **E**vidence, **E**xplanation.

- Ask the students to get into pairs. Each pair should choose a quotation. They should write the opening point on their whiteboards (remembering to end the point with a colon). They then write the quote and pass the whiteboard to another pair, who must write the explanation.

- Ask the students to share their explanations with the rest of the group.

Personal paragraph organisers 1

Objective covered

Sn10 *Recognise how sentences are organised in a paragraph in which the content is not chronological, e.g. by comparison.*

Aim

To identify what a paragraph does and how it is organised.
To practise writing a topic sentence supported by two or three sentences which add detail and exemplification.

Activity

- Remind the students that a paragraph is made up of a series of sentences about the same topic or key idea. It is organised around the topic sentence which states clearly what the whole paragraph is about. This is often followed by supporting sentences that give further information.

- Display this information text:

  > Stalactites and stalagmites are formed inside limestone caves. The water that drips steadily from the roof contains a mineral called calcite. The water dries but the calcite remains and slowly builds up into a column. Stalactites grow downwards from the cave roof. Stalagmites grow upwards from the cave floor. Sometimes the two columns meet to form a pillar.

- Ask the students to identify the topic sentence. Then discuss what the remaining five sentences do.

- Now give the students the following topic sentence and ask them to create a sequence of supporting sentences to complete the paragraph:

  > Satellite television is becoming a standard feature of many households.

Personal paragraph organisers 2

Objective covered

Sn10 *Recognise how sentences are organised in a paragraph in which the content is not chronological, e.g. by comparison.*

Aim

To identify what a paragraph does and how it is organised. To practise writing a topic sentence supported by two or three sentences which add detail and exemplification.

Activity

- Display the following topic sentence and bullet points:

  Some people think that watching sport on TV is not as good as going to the stadium and seeing it live.

  - Live atmosphere
  - Financial support for the sport
  - Social activity
  - Too crowded
  - Too expensive
  - Inconvenient

- Ask the students to work in small groups. They should construct a series of sentences around the bullet points to build up into a paragraph.

Pulling things together 1

Objective covered
Sn6 *Compare and use different ways of opening, developing, linking and completing paragraphs.*

Aim
To explore the cohesive devices appropriate to letter writing.

Activity
❀ Display this text:

The do-it-yourself multi-purpose thank you letter

Dear _____

I am writing to thank you for the wonderful _____ that you sent me for Christmas/my birthday/a joke.

I was especially pleased to receive it because _____.

It will be particularly useful for _____ as long as _____.

Alternatively it will come in handy when _____ or if I ever need _____.

Although _____, it was exactly what I wanted.

Moreover it _____ which will certainly impress all my classmates.

Finally, can I just say how much _____.

Yours _____

❀ Ask the students to work with partners to provide the most apt or amusing text to fill in the gaps. You could begin by tackling the first couple of gaps as a whole class.

❀ After five or ten minutes, take suggestions to compile a shared version.

❀ Complete the activity by returning to the original grid. Ask the students to explain how the grid works. (It is a frame that provides connectives and other phrases or clauses that hold the text together.)

Pulling things together 2

YEAR 9

Objective covered

Sn6 *Compare and use different ways of opening, developing, linking and completing paragraphs.*

Aim

To explore cohesive devices appropriate to particular types of letter.

Activity

⊛ Display the text used in 'Pulling things together 1', page 61 (The do-it-yourself multi-purpose thank you letter).

⊛ Briefly recap on the features of such a frame, emphasising the role of connectives. If possible, refer to a list or display of connectives that can be used to develop a text. (A very useful list is provided as Handout 3.1 in the *Key Stage 3 National Strategy Literacy Across the Curriculum* folder.)

⊛ Ask the students to work in pairs. Each student has five minutes to write their own frame choosing from one of these options:

- the do-it-yourself multi-purpose letter of complaint

- the do-it-yourself multi-purpose love letter

- the do-it-yourself multi-purpose begging letter (e.g. to raise funds).

⊛ The students should then swap letter frames with their partners. They now need to write with a different coloured pen or pencil to fill in the gaps.

⊛ Finished texts can be used to support a display on connectives or writing style.

What's my style?

Objective covered

Sn8 *Know and use effectively the vocabulary, sentence grammar and stylistic conventions of the writing forms featured in specific subjects during the current year.*

Aim

To recognise and use the conventions of writing forms from different subjects.

Activity

✸ Display the following:

- A small quantity of copper sulphate crystals were heated in a test tube over a high flame.

- Me and Andy whacked some of this blue stuff into a glass tube thing and heated it up.

✸ Ask the students to identify what the two texts are. (An appropriate and an inappropriate science text.)

✸ Now ask the students to create an appropriate and an inappropriate sentence for any subject area. They should then share examples with the class.

In the style of...

Objective covered/aim

Sn9 *Adapt the stylistic conventions of the main non-fiction text types to fit different audiences and purposes, e.g. advertisements, documentaries, editorials.*

Activity

⊛ Write a list of non-fiction text types on the board, for example: news report, advertisement, diary, reference book, instruction manual, business letter.

⊛ Pick a well-known story from a fairy tale or nursery rhyme, such as *The Three Little Pigs*, *Humpty Dumpty*, *Goldilocks* or *Red Riding Hood*.

⊛ Each student chooses (or is given) one of the text types listed. They then have to write a short extract (e.g. four sentences) in that style, relating to the agreed story. Other students then have to guess which is the chosen text type. As an illustration, you might choose *The Three Little Pigs* and write a few sentences from:

- a TV news bulletin on domestic violence
- a set of numbered instructions on how to catch a big, bad wolf
- a persuasive letter from the wolf to the pigs (arguing that he is a peaceful vegetarian and that they should trust him and admit him to their homes)
- an entry from a reference book giving a brief biography (Wolf, Big Bad, 1990–2002)
- a diary entry by one of the pigs, revealing their anxiety.

Differentiation

⊛ ⇑ Once the game has been established, groups could play this independently. A more confident group could play this without a prescribed list of text types and extend the range to include any non-fiction genre for the others to guess.

⊛ ⇓ This game could initially be modelled through shared writing.

Notice this

Objective covered

Sn10 *Identify the key alterations made to a text when it is changed from an informal to a formal text, e.g. change from first to third person, nominalisation, use of passive verbs.*

Aim

To identify and experiment with the features of formal and official texts.

Activity

⊛ Display this notice:

> Owing to circumstances beyond our control, these stairs are unavailable for public use.
>
> Students are requested to avail themselves of the window facilities.

⊛ Then display this informal translation:

> The stairs are closed. Jump out of the window!

⊛ Investigate and identify the features that make a notice impersonal and official.

⊛ Next ask the students to write their own spoof notices plus their own informal translations.

Differentiation

⊛ ⇑ Compose other formal documents and their informal 'translations'. Confrontational scenarios are particularly rewarding here (e.g. a school report of someone who has done no work; a letter sacking somebody).

Follow up

⊛ Use ICT to design the notices – this adds a further degree of authority to a notice. Finished versions can be annotated to form a display about the features of official language.

Style guru 1

Objective covered

Sn7 *Analyse and exploit the stylistic conventions of the main text types, e.g. parody.*

Aim

To explore satirical presentations of recognisable stylistic conventions through a speaking and listening activity.

Activity

⊛ Ask the class to brainstorm the features of *Blue Peter* presenters' way of talking. For example, they are clear, focused, good-humoured, encouraging, upbeat. Model packing a school bag in the style of a *Blue Peter* presenter. You could start with:

> 'Hello everybody! Well, this afternoon I am going to show you how packing a school bag can be *really* easy and fun. Now, you don't need to have special skills – anyone can do it. It's always a good idea to think about the things you will need and have them ready to pack. Here are some things I prepared earlier: books, PE kit, pencil case and packed lunch – mustn't forget the packed lunch! Now I am going to show you just how *easy* it is.'

⊛ Give the students the following list of recognisable stylistic types:

- news reader
- football commentator
- *Crimewatch* presenter
- headteacher in assembly.

⊛ Ask the students to get into pairs. They should prepare their own version of packing a school bag in one of the given styles.

Follow up

⊛ The above starter can be developed as a polished improvisation. For example, students may wish to devise whole interviews.

Style guru 2

Objective covered

Sn7 *Analyse and exploit the stylistic conventions of the main text types, e.g. parody.*

Aim

To develop the activity from 'Style guru 1', page 66, so that students can explore written conventions of parody.

Resources

Individual whiteboards and pens.

Activity

⊛ Recall the activity from 'Style guru 1', page 66, and quickly brainstorm the spoken stylistic conventions of TV newsreaders.

⊛ Ask the students to write a headline TV news report on a very trivial subject, for example: a school student loses a pencil; a dustbin has been knocked over in Shaftesbury.

Follow up

⊛ Develop this activity by inviting students to devise a full piece of writing. There are a number of fun permutations, for example writing on serious topics in the style of Homer Simpson, one of Harry Enfield's characters or a character from a soap opera.

Talking posh

Objective covered

Sn15 *Vary the formality of language in speech and writing to suit different circumstances.*

Aim

To encourage students to vary vocabulary, intonation and sentence structure in order to suit audience and purpose.

Activity

- Ask the students to think of examples of formal and informal greetings, for example 'How do you do?' or 'Hi there!'

- Write the following dialogue on the board:

    'Look mate, that banger you flogged me the other day is a right heap of rubbish.'

    'Don't talk daft. At that price I was giving it away!'

- Invite students to continue the next two sentences of the dialogue, using informal language.

- Ask the students to convert this into formal English.

Follow up

- Continue the above as an improvised drama activity.

- Ask the students to write a formal letter to the car company.

68

Um...er

Objective covered

Sn16 *Investigate differences between spoken and written language structures, e.g. hesitation in speech.*

Aim

To explore the differences of language use in speaking and writing.

Activity

⊛ Display the following:

> 'Um...hello...are you busy? ...I...I...was wondering
> if I could have a quick word?...um...I...er...wanted
> to...wanted to...to have a chat about the car I got
> from you...er...the other day.'

⊛ Ask the students why this is an example of spoken English.
Draw out the following points: hesitation, repetition, slang.

⊛ Ask the students to convert the example into written
English. They should read their work to the rest of the
class. You should focus on formal language structures that
work well.

Follow up

⊛ In order to illustrate how spoken
English differs from written
structures, the class could play *Just
a minute,* where they have to talk
on a subject without hesitation,
repetition or deviation.

Writing posh

Objective covered

Sn17 *Use standard English consistently in formal situations and in writing.*

Aim

To explore ways of expressing formality in writing.

Activity

⊛ Tell the students that they are going to compose some sentences that could be included in a formal letter of complaint. Model an example of an opening sentence, for example:

> It is with great regret that I write to convey my disappointment with the car I purchased from you on 14 February.

⊛ Divide the class into five groups. Allocate each group a paragraph from the list below.

- Paragraph 1: Introduce yourself and remind the owner of what happened when you visited the garage recently.
- Paragraph 2: Outline what exactly went wrong with the car.
- Paragraph 3: Describe your family's reaction.
- Paragraph 4: Describe how inconvenient it is not to have a reliable car.
- Paragraph 5: Explain what further action you intend to take if you are not given your money back.

They should write the topic sentence for their allocated paragraph in formal English.

⊛ Ask each group to read out their examples. Comment on the use of standard English.

Follow up

⊛ The students could write the whole letter.

Ye Olde Englishe

Objective covered/aim

Sn18 *Identify specific ways sentence structure and punctuation are different in older texts.*

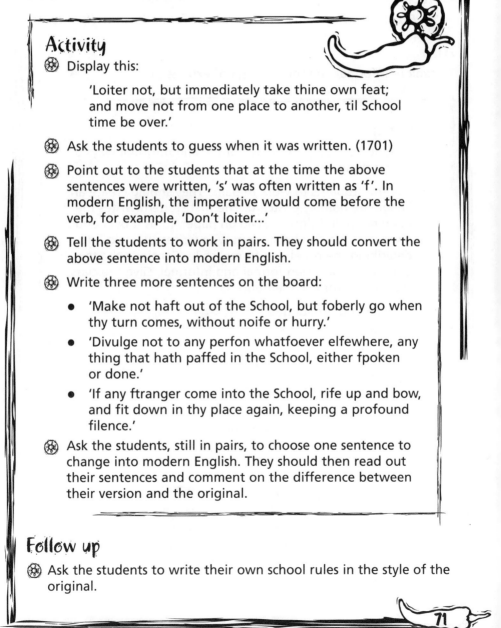

Activity

❀ Display this:

> 'Loiter not, but immediately take thine own feat; and move not from one place to another, til School time be over.'

❀ Ask the students to guess when it was written. (1701)

❀ Point out to the students that at the time the above sentences were written, 's' was often written as 'f'. In modern English, the imperative would come before the verb, for example, 'Don't loiter...'

❀ Tell the students to work in pairs. They should convert the above sentence into modern English.

❀ Write three more sentences on the board:

- 'Make not haft out of the School, but foberly go when thy turn comes, without noife or hurry.'
- 'Divulge not to any perfon whatfoever elfewhere, any thing that hath paffed in the School, either fpoken or done.'
- 'If any ftranger come into the School, rife up and bow, and fit down in thy place again, keeping a profound filence.'

❀ Ask the students, still in pairs, to choose one sentence to change into modern English. They should then read out their sentences and comment on the difference between their version and the original.

Follow up

❀ Ask the students to write their own school rules in the style of the original.

Postcard consequences

Objective covered

Sn12 *Explore and use different degrees of formality in written texts.*

Aim

To explore informal and formal ways of expression.

Activity

- ✸ Remind the students about formal and informal ways of saying things.

- ✸ Ask the students to work in pairs. They should create an imaginary holiday postcard. The first student writes the opening in an informal style on paper, folds it over and gives it to the second student who writes the next line, describing the hotel in a formal style. Continue the text, alternating between formal and informal. Give the class the subject for each sentence:

  - Opening/greeting
  - Hotel
  - Weather
  - Entertainment
  - What you miss about home
  - Signing off

- ✸ Invite the students to read out their postcards.

Show some attitude

Objective covered / aim

Sn10 *Explore different attitudes to language, and identify characteristics of standard English that make it the dominant mode of public communication.*

Activity

⊛ Begin by reminding the students that there are a great many varieties of spoken English. This is mostly determined by where people come from, but there are other factors (e.g. fashion).

⊛ Ask the students to work in pairs or small groups. Each group has to come up with a list of statements about the way other people speak English. Each statement has to begin:

> 'I really like the way some people...'
> or 'I can't stand the way some people...'

Statements might relate to:

- different accents or dialects
- particular words or expressions
- particular types of discourse (weather forecasting, advertisements, sports commentaries).

⊛ After a while, collect examples from different groups. Ask other students to vote using thumbs up or down to show the extent of their agreement with each statement.

⊛ Conclude by asking all the students to use the thumbs up/down response to these statements:

- as long as someone can be understood, it doesn't matter how they say it
- some versions of English are better than others
- everyone has their own prejudices about language
- criticism about other people's English is always snobbery.

Follow up

⊛ This activity could lead to a debate or essay on the subjects.

Brave new words

Objective covered

Sn11 *Investigate ways English has changed over time and identify current trends of language change, e.g. word meanings.*

Aim

To investigate how new words enter the English lexicon.

Activity

⚙ This is best used when students are studying a pre-twentieth century text where some of the outdated vocabulary makes demands on the reader, such as Shakespeare or Chaucer.

⚙ Ask the students to work individually or in pairs. They should make a list of ten words or phrases that Shakespeare would not have understood, for example:

> skateboard, astronaut, nuclear, atomic, photograph

⚙ Now ask them to make a second list of ten words or phrases that nobody would have understood twenty years ago, for example:

> text message, Internet, Game Boy, PlayStation

⚙ They should aim to end up without any word appearing on both lists.

Hint

⚙ Tell students who find this task difficult to think about technology and fashion. (e.g. List 1: car, bicycle, television, e-mail; List 2: wicked = good)

Fact finders

Objective covered

R1 *Know how to locate resources for a given task, and find relevant information in them, e.g. skimming, use of index, glossary, key words, hotlinks.*

Aim

To revise and consolidate students' use of appropriate reading strategies.

Resources

A set of any one non-fiction text, such as information books, leaflets, brochures or textbooks from any school subject.

Activity

❀ Divide the class into teams. Allow a fixed time, say five minutes, for the students to set questions based on the text for other teams to answer. The only rule is that it must be possible to work out the answer by using the text.

❀ At the end of the preparation time, use the questions for a quiz. Either split the class into small teams who challenge one another or choose some of the questions for the whole class to answer.

Differentiation

❀ ⇑ More confident readers can be encouraged to set questions that go beyond information retrieval, such as questions that require inference and deduction.

Speedy notes 1

Objective covered/aim

R3 *Increase the speed and accuracy of note-making skills.*

Resources

Short extract from *Happy Days with the Naked Chef* by Jamie Oliver.
Individual whiteboards and pens.

Activity

⊛ Ask a student to read out the following extract from the book jacket. Model making bullet points to answer: 'Why are Jamie Oliver's cookbooks so popular?'

> Jamie believes in finding the best ingredients and making tasty, easy, sociable food with the minimum of fuss. Like his first two books, *Happy Days* is filled with fantastic salads, pastas, meat, fish, breads and deserts for all occasions. Along with his perfect curry for a night in, he gives you his version of some old favourites in 'Comfort Grub' – try his Steak and Guinness Pie or indulge in his to-die-for pancakes! And in 'Quick Fixes' he whips up some really simple, tasty dinners – just right when you come home late from work.

⊛ Your five bullet points could be: 'Tasty food', 'Easy to make', 'Variety of recipes', 'Quick', 'Suitable for all occasions'.

⊛ Ask the students to make three bullet points as you read the next extract. These are to answer: 'Why is this cookery book suitable for children?'

> The 'Kids' Club' chapter is all about catching kids' attention and getting them interested in food. It's a starting point for children, to encourage them to have a go at other things in the book with their parents. Get them squashing tomatoes, pouring olive oil, pitting olives and making bread in no time – they'll love it.

Speedy notes 2

Objective covered
R3 *Increase the speed and accuracy of note-making skills and use notes for re-presenting information for specific purposes.*

Aim
For students to re-present the material from 'Speedy notes 1', page 76, in the form of a spider diagram.

Resources
Individual whiteboards and pens.

Activity
⊛ Reread the first extract from 'Speedy notes 1', page 76.

⊛ Model how you would construct a spider diagram from the information you selected and some additional points:

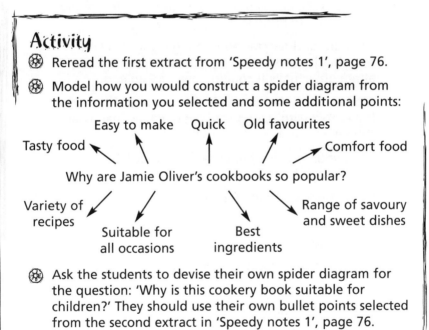

Easy to make   Quick   Old favourites

Tasty food ↖   ↑   ↑   ↗   ➤ Comfort food

Why are Jamie Oliver's cookbooks so popular?

Variety of recipes ↙   ↙   ↘   ➤ Range of savoury and sweet dishes

Suitable for all occasions   Best ingredients

⊛ Ask the students to devise their own spider diagram for the question: 'Why is this cookery book suitable for children?' They should use their own bullet points selected from the second extract in 'Speedy notes 1', page 76.

⊛ Select students to show and describe their diagrams to the whole group.

Follow up
⊛ Ask the students to write a piece for a Jamie Oliver cookbook jacket using their own words.

What are you implying?

Objective covered/aim

R8 *Infer and deduce meanings using evidence in the text, identifying where and how meanings are implied.*

Activity

✸ Display this text extract or give a copy to each pair of students. It is from *The Box* by Ann Cameron, a story intended for younger children. Explain that the character narrating the story has been told that there is an animal of some kind in the box and he and his brother are waiting for their father to bring it in.

> We waited. Huey started rubbing his special laser ring that is supposed to fry your enemies to a crisp, although actually it couldn't even fry an egg.
>
> Gloria and my father set the box down in front of us. It was tied with strong cord. I moved my feet away from it.
>
> 'Now your job,' my father said to us, 'will be to open this box.'
>
> 'O.K.,' Huey said, rubbing his ring.
>
> 'I don't want to,' I said.
>
> Gloria looked at me sympathetically.

✸ Ask the students to use two different colours to highlight words or phrases that:

- hint at what might be inside the box
- hint at how the characters are feeling.

Differentiation

✸ ⇑ Ask the students to continue the text by writing the next three lines, basing what they write on the inferences they have made from the text.

Take any advert

Objective covered/aim

R10 *Identify how media texts are tailored to suit their audience, and recognise that audience responses vary, e.g. popular websites.*

Resources

Examples of advertisements from any branch of the media.
Individual whiteboards and pens.

Activity

⊛ Present any advertisement to the students. Model how you would analyse it by using the following questions:

- What is it selling? (e.g. content)
- Who is the audience? (e.g. children, women, men, occupations, age)
- How is it presented? (e.g. visual images, colour, font, titles, logos, sound effects, music)
- What special language has been used? (e.g. jingles, slogans, puns, colloquial, formal, figurative, abbreviations, questions, statistics, repetition, imperatives)

⊛ Once you have done the above, the students will be ready to try their own analysis, once again, with any advertisement. Ask them to work in pairs and record their initial responses on their whiteboards.

⊛ The basis for students' feedback will be: 'Is the advertisement persuasive?' This will allow the students to explore and compare their personal responses.

Hint

⊛ When using TV advertisements, try to tape two consecutively at a certain time of day. The above works well with adverts taped between 6:30 am and 11:30 am at weekends. These are primarily aimed at children and present rich possibilities for quick analysis.

Is that a fact?

Objective covered

R6 *Recognise bias and objectivity, distinguishing facts from hypotheses, theories or opinions.*

Aim

To reinforce and develop students' understanding of what is a fact and what is an opinion.

Activity

- ⊛ Display the following:

  - I love school.

  - I have PE twice a week.

  - *Eastenders* is rubbish.

  - West Ham United is the best.

  - Rome is the capital of Italy.

- ⊛ Read each statement out and ask the students to vote for 'fact' or 'opinion'. Ask them to give reasons.

- ⊛ Ask the students to work in pairs. They should think of one fact and one opinion to do with the theme of pop music.

- ⊛ Each pair should then share their examples with the class. The other students should vote for which is fact and which is opinion.

Differentiation

- ⊛ ⇑ The students should think of statements to do with another theme, for example school or sport.

Follow up

- ⊛ Ask the students to carry out an analysis of a tabloid newspaper article. They should highlight facts and opinions in different colours.

What's in the news?

Objective covered

R8 *Analyse how media texts influence and are influenced by readers, e.g. interactive programmes, selection of news items.*

Aim

To analyse and create tabloid and broadsheet headlines.

Activity

⊛ Display the following headlines:
  - PRINCE FINDS SOLE-MATE!
  - PRINCE TO MARRY CINDERELLA AFTER UNUSUAL COURTSHIP.

⊛ Ask the students to identify which comes from a tabloid newspaper and which from a broadsheet. They should identify language features that create impact and therefore influence the reader.

⊛ Tell the students to work in pairs. They should create tabloid and broadsheet headlines for one of the following stories:
  - *Little Red Riding Hood*
  - *Goldilocks*
  - *Sleeping Beauty*
  - *The Beauty and the Beast*

⊛ They should then share their headlines with the whole class.

Differentiation

⊛ ⇑ Encourage the students to use bias in their headlines so that conventional responses to recognisable characters are changed. For instance, they could present Cinderella as an attention-seeking and selfish sister who ruined her sisters' evening by turning up at the ball.

Follow up

⊛ Ask the students to write two articles: one in the style of a broadsheet and one in the style of a tabloid.

Horror story

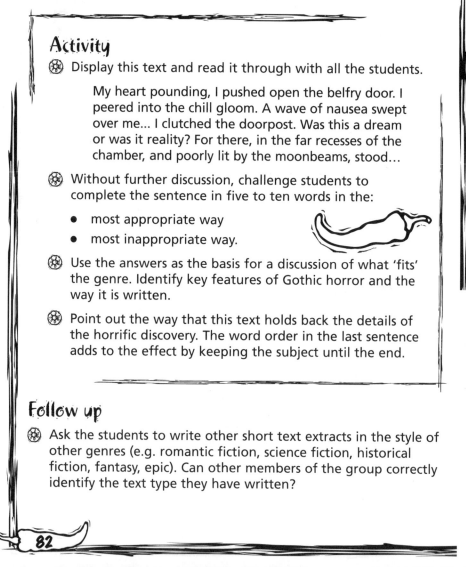

Objective covered

R14 *Recognise the conventions of some common literary forms, e.g. sonnet, and genres, e.g. Gothic horror, and explore how a particular text adheres to or deviates from established conventions.*

Aim

To identify and imitate the features of Gothic horror fiction.

Activity

❀ Display this text and read it through with all the students.

> My heart pounding, I pushed open the belfry door. I peered into the chill gloom. A wave of nausea swept over me... I clutched the doorpost. Was this a dream or was it reality? For there, in the far recesses of the chamber, and poorly lit by the moonbeams, stood...

❀ Without further discussion, challenge students to complete the sentence in five to ten words in the:

- most appropriate way
- most inappropriate way.

❀ Use the answers as the basis for a discussion of what 'fits' the genre. Identify key features of Gothic horror and the way it is written.

❀ Point out the way that this text holds back the details of the horrific discovery. The word order in the last sentence adds to the effect by keeping the subject until the end.

Follow up

❀ Ask the students to write other short text extracts in the style of other genres (e.g. romantic fiction, science fiction, historical fiction, fantasy, epic). Can other members of the group correctly identify the text type they have written?

Story consequences

Objective covered
Wr5 *Structure a story with an arresting opening, a developing plot, a complication, a crisis and a satisfying resolution.*

Aim
To understand the essentials of story structure in a consequences-style game.

Resources
Use either blank sheets of paper or prepare copies of sheets giving these key sentence starters:

- The story is set in...
- The main character(s) is/are...
- The big problem is...
- Things get worse when...
- Things get even worse when...
- The real crisis is when...
- The resolution is...
- At the very end we see...

Activity

- Each student starts with the sheet and completes the first sentence stem giving brief details of where and when the story is set, for example in a spaceship in a faraway galaxy; in a secondary school one Friday at the end of the last lesson. Give a strict time limit.

- The sheets should be passed on but not folded over. Students now receive someone else's story setting and add details of one or two characters to fit the setting, giving brief descriptions (not just their names).

- The plans are passed on again as students complicate the storylines.

- The final prompt is designed to show that stories usually conclude with a scene showing what the events mean to the characters or the community. For example: the village celebrating the death of the dragon; a wedding; the start of a new school term.

Introducing...

Objective covered

Wr6 *Portray character, directly and indirectly, through description, dialogue and action.*

Aim

To portray a character concisely and indirectly.

Activity

* Use this brief text as a model. Adapt it to fit the class. Display:

> The classroom door swung open and the new supply teacher strode in.
>
> 'Siddown,' she snarled, spitting out the end of a Cuban cigar as she scanned the room.
>
> 'C-c-crikey,' whispered Daniel. 'She's mean, real mean.'

* Investigate the ways in which the author has quickly conveyed the character of the supply teacher:

  * the writer's description (conveyed indirectly through strong verbs and the adverbial clause)
  * the teacher's actions
  * what she says
  * the way others react to and speak about her.

* Now ask the students to write their own three-sentence introduction of a new character. They should use strong verbs, for example instead of 'walked', they could use 'strode', 'stumbled', 'leaped', 'skipped' and so on. They should also use adverbial phrases like 'with a cruel sneer' or clauses like 'swinging from the chandelier'.

Give us a clue

Objective covered

Wr7 *Use a range of narrative devices to involve the reader, e.g. withholding information.*

Aim

To investigate and use a narrative device to 'hook' the reader.

Activity

✿ Display these sentences:

- As Tom fumbled for his door key, he barely noticed the stranger at the bus stop on the other side of the street.
- For some reason, even before she went into the house, Nadia felt frightened.
- If I had known then what Jamie was really like, I would never have trusted him.

✿ Ask the students to identify the kind of texts they are. They are all recounts, probably fiction and many students might call them cliffhangers or turning points. Each one raises a question like 'Who/what is the stranger?' and/or hints at trouble ahead.

✿ Tell the students to write one sentence that could be the last sentence of a chapter. It should aim to 'hook' the reader by raising a question and hinting at danger or problems ahead.

Differentiation

✿ ⇓ Provide a bank of useful phrases to start sentences:

- Just as…
- If only…
- It was only when…
- Apart from…

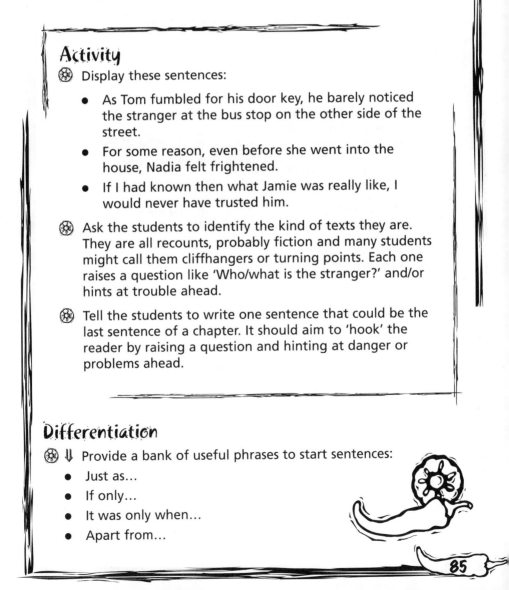

Sound effects

Objective covered

Wr8 *Experiment with the visual and sound effects of language, including the use of imagery, alliteration, rhythm and rhyme.*

Aim

To increase familiarity with different language effects.

Activity

✹ Display these two lists and ask the students to match the quotes with the names of language effects.

1 He cut through the defence like a knife through butter.	**A** Rhyme and rhythm
	B Visual effect
2 A blanket of fog wrapped up the village.	**C** Metaphor
	D Alliteration
3 She looked mean, moody and magnificent.	**E** Simile
4 The rain in Spain Falls mainly on the plain.	
5 The falcon s	

        w

          o

           o

            p

              ed to seize its prey.

✹ Ask the students to write five quotes like the ones above, with no more than one example of each language effect. These should then be used for a quiz.

Answers

1E, 2C, 3D, 4A, 5B

My love is like...

Objective covered

Wr6 *Experiment with figurative language in conveying a sense of character and setting.*

Aim

To use simile to describe objects or settings and to justify the choices made in doing so.

Activity

- Display the following line from *My Love is Like a Red, Red, Rose*, the Robbie Burns poem.

    > My love is like a red, red rose, that's newly sprung in June.

- Remind or ask the students about similes and what they do. The students think for a few moments about what Burns is trying to convey about his love by describing it in this way. Share ideas.

- Now students, either in pairs or individually, should create their own simile descriptions for people and places. They should be prepared to explain their intention as authors in using the simile. For example:

    - My room is like a calm, green oasis.
      'I chose this simile because my room is my special place where I go after the trials of a busy day.'
    - My desk is like a city after the bombs have fallen.
      'I chose this simile because my workspace is a real mess.'

Differentiation

- ⇑ Move from simile into metaphor by asking the students to restructure their sentences to remove the 'like' or 'as', for example: the oasis that is my bedroom; the bombsite of my desk.

Changing rooms 1

Objective covered

Wr6 *Experiment with figurative language in conveying a sense of character and setting.*

Aim

To explore how metaphors can add depth and meaning when creating a setting.

Activity

⊛ Remind the students that a metaphor is a phrase which compares one thing to another without using the words 'like' or 'as'. Explain that writers use metaphors to make the setting in their stories more vivid.

⊛ Pick up, or point to, objects in the classroom and invite students to think of comparisons using metaphors. For example, a spider plant is:

- a firework exploding
- someone having a bad hair day
- a new star being born
- a volcano erupting.

⊛ Ask the students to picture their bedrooms and write down three things they see. With a partner, they should decide on metaphors to describe these things. For example, 'My computer is a criminal that steals my time.' Ask them to share their metaphors with the class.

Changing rooms 2

Objective covered

Wr9 *Experiment with presenting similar material in different forms and styles of poetry.*

Aim

To develop ideas from 'Changing rooms 1', page 88, by encouraging students to apply their figurative material in haiku poetry.

Activity

※ Remind the students how a haiku is written. They have three lines: line one has 5 syllables; line two has 7 syllables; line three has 5 syllables.

※ Model the following example on the board:

> Computers are fiends,
> Robbing us of our spare time.
> They wait eagerly.

※ Note the opening line, which is a metaphor, and the way it has been personified in the rest of the poem.

※ Ask the students to work in pairs. They should use their metaphors from 'Changing rooms 1', page 88, to compose a haiku together.

※ Invite pairs to read out their examples to the class.

Follow up

※ Pupils can use their metaphors in free verse rather than haiku.

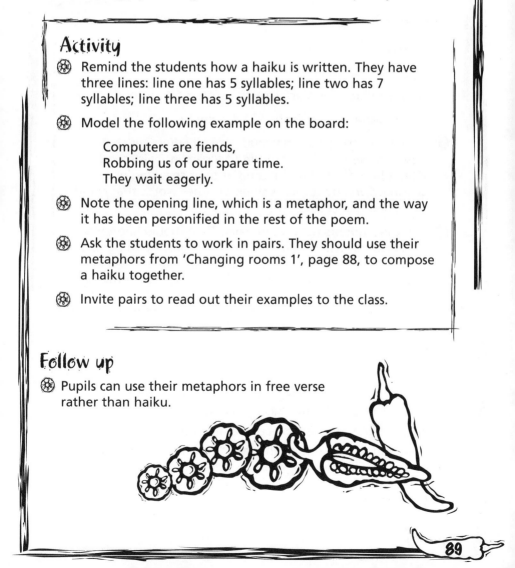

In the mood

Objective covered

Wr7 *Experiment with different language choices to imply meaning and to establish the tone of a piece, e.g. ironic, indignant.*

Aim

To make choices about words and style to set the intended tone for a piece of writing.

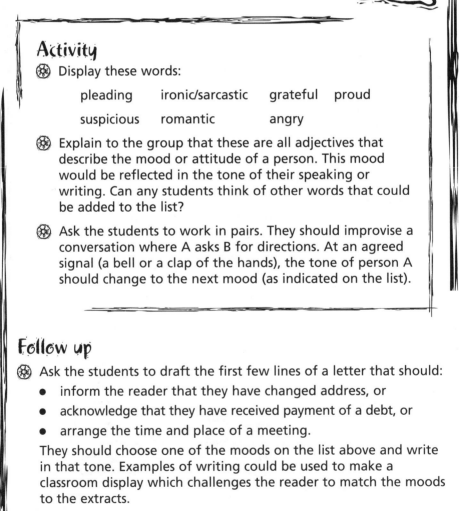

Activity

⊛ Display these words:

>   pleading   ironic/sarcastic   grateful   proud
>
>   suspicious   romantic   angry

⊛ Explain to the group that these are all adjectives that describe the mood or attitude of a person. This mood would be reflected in the tone of their speaking or writing. Can any students think of other words that could be added to the list?

⊛ Ask the students to work in pairs. They should improvise a conversation where A asks B for directions. At an agreed signal (a bell or a clap of the hands), the tone of person A should change to the next mood (as indicated on the list).

Follow up

⊛ Ask the students to draft the first few lines of a letter that should:

- inform the reader that they have changed address, or
- acknowledge that they have received payment of a debt, or
- arrange the time and place of a meeting.

They should choose one of the moods on the list above and write in that tone. Examples of writing could be used to make a classroom display which challenges the reader to match the moods to the extracts.

Storylines

YEAR 8

Objective covered

Wr8 *Develop an imaginative or unusual treatment of familiar material or established conventions, e.g. updating traditional tales.*

Aim

To retell a well-known narrative in an unlikely genre.

Activity

⊛ Display this list of narrative genres:

- romance
- crime
- horror
- science fiction
- historical

Can students think of any others?

⊛ Choose a familiar tale or nursery rhyme, for example *Jack and Jill*. Demonstrate how to retell part of the narrative in one of the genres. Illustrate romance:

> Jack looked wistfully at Jill. It was a beautiful day and the startling blue of the sky mirrored the brightness of his sweetheart's eyes. Taking her tenderly by the hand, he set off up the hill.

⊛ The students should retell a short section of a story in their chosen genre.

Follow up

⊛ The students could make a children's storybook by writing the same story repeatedly but in different genres.

First lines, last lines

Objective covered
Wr5 *Explore different ways of opening, structuring and ending narratives.*

Aim
To explore openings and endings of narrative writing genres by responding to a variety of initial stimuli.

Activity

⊛ Display the following final line of a story:

> At last, Cleo and Winston walked hand in hand into the sunset.

⊛ Ask the students to work in pairs. They should write a possible opening line for the ending above.

⊛ Take feedback and share ideas, brainstorming as many ideas about the romantic genre as possible.

⊛ Ask the students to write opening lines to match the following last lines:

- Striking the last blow, he knew that Baroness Von Gibaud would never darken his castle doors again.
- Jason had come home at last.
- Kate clutched her prize, vowing that this was the happiest day of her life.

⊛ Students should share their opening lines with the whole group.

Follow up

⊛ Play a game where students begin by creating the first and last lines of a story. These are then mixed up and displayed so that other students can match them.

⊛ This activity lends itself to narrative writing projects, the next stage being the creation of the summary of the story that goes in between the first and last lines.

Different voices

Objective covered
Wr5 *Experiment with narrative perspective.*

Aim
To explore a variety of narrative voices and understand the impact a change of voice can have on a story's perspective.

Activity
⊛ Read out the following text. Invite students to guess what story is being told and by which character:

> 'Let me tell you, if my feet had been one size smaller, right now I'd be living in the lap of luxury.'

(Answer: an ugly sister retells *Cinderella*.)

⊛ Ask the students to choose a character from any familiar text (e.g. a traditional tale, a well-known film, a class novel or play). They should then say something in the style of their chosen character and see if others can guess the narrator.

Follow up
⊛ Students could choose one of the characters from the above activity and write a diary or letter recounting the story using the first person narrative.

Wish you were here

Objective covered

Wr7 *Explore how non-fiction texts can convey information or ideas in amusing or entertaining ways.*

Aim

To investigate and implement language devices (e.g. exaggeration) to make non-fiction writing entertaining.

Activity

※ Display these extracts. Ask the students if they can work out the source (or the sort of book they might come from).

- 'Bradford's role in life is to make every place else in the world look better in comparison, and it does this very well.'

- 'Corfe is a popular and pretty place, a cluster of stone cottages dominated by the lofty, jagged walls of its famous and much-photographed castle...'

- 'Well, all I can say is that Blackpool's illuminations are nothing if not splendid, and they are not splendid.'

- 'I spent a pleasant night in Lincoln, wandering its steep and ancient streets before and after dinner, admiring the squat, dark immensity of the cathedral and its two gothic towers.'

The extracts are all from *Notes from a Small Island*, a travel book by Bill Bryson.

※ Ask the students to work in pairs. They should compose two descriptions of the place where they live (or of a local town)

- one which is negative and funny
- one which is positive and descriptive.

※ Students should share their descriptions with the group.

Follow up

※ This activity lends itself to further work on guidebooks and travel writing.

Where next?

Objective covered
Wr14 *Develop and signpost arguments in ways that make the logic clear to the reader.*

Aim
To use connective phrases clearly and appropriately.

Resources
Individual whiteboards and pens.

Activity

- Remind the students of the kinds of connectives used for developing an argument. Create a short class speech on the subject 'I think fox-hunting is wrong'. Ask the students, on their whiteboards, to write responses to the following connective phrases first. Explain the role of each phrase first:
  - For example (give an example as to why fox-hunting is wrong)
  - On the other hand (give an opposing view)
  - However (develop your personal point of view giving an example)
  - In addition to this (another point which develops the last one)
  - Finally (sum up your opinion)
- Divide the students into groups of five. Each member of the group should choose one of the above connective phrases.
- Give the class the following subject: 'Smoking should be banned in public places.' The first group member should write down the opening statement: 'I think smoking should/should not be banned in public places. For example...' The second group member should continue by writing 'On the other hand...' and so on.
- The groups should present their final pieces to the class.

On the contrary

YEAR 9

Objective covered

Wr14 *Make a counter-argument to a view that has been expressed, addressing weaknesses in the argument and offering alternatives.*

Aim

To use connectives to develop a line of thinking and to create a counter-argument to a view given.

Activity

- Write the following list of connective devices on the board:
  - On the contrary
  - I would disagree because
  - Although
  - Despite
  - Even so
  - However
  - An alternative point of view would be

- Identify these as connectives that signal an opposition or an alteration to a point of view.

- Ask the students to listen to the following point of view and tell them that they will need to create a counter-argument to this point of view:

    Teenagers should not be allowed to have part-time jobs. It interferes with their homework and exam preparation. Part-time work often leaves them too exhausted either to study properly or to take part in those sports activities needed to maintain health.

- Give the students five minutes to prepare and then share outcomes.

Follow up

- Use the same technique, combined with some teacher modelling, as a basis for formal presentations and debates using standard English.

What's my name?

Objective covered

S&L1 *Use talk as a tool for clarifying ideas, e.g. by articulating problems or asking pertinent questions.*

Aim

To improve students' questioning skills.

Resources

Sticky labels or Post-it notes.

Activity

❊ Prepare a label with the name of a famous person to stick on the back (or forehead) of each student playing. Each player then has to move around the room and discover their 'identity' by asking questions that can only be answered 'yes' or 'no'. Each player can only ask one question of any other player and then must move on.

❊ A discussion of the game will need to consider the kind of questions that work best. For example, the value of questions about categories of people (e.g. 'Am I fictional?', 'Am I alive?', 'Am I British?') rather than random guesses.

❊ Further versions of the game can be used to serve other objectives, for example:

- Every name is a character from fiction read by the class.
- Simply use random words (e.g. 'cupboard', 'slowly'). Here students will need to use other terms to narrow down their search (e.g. names of word classes: 'Am I a noun?', 'Am I an adverb?').
- Use subject-specific terms (e.g. names from history; locations from geography; materials or chemicals from science).
- Give blank labels to the students and ask them to supply the names.

Words in action

Objective covered/aim

S&L4 *Provide an explanation or commentary which links words with actions or images, e.g. a sports commentary or talking to a sequence of images.*

Resources

You might want to show a clip from a sports event so that students can see and hear how the commentary matches the action.

Activity

⊛ Group the students in pairs or trios. Ask them to spend a minute discussing what they think might be the challenges faced by a journalist commentating on a live event (e.g. live sports match, the State opening of Parliament, a Royal occasion, the voice-over to a live concert). Take feedback.

⊛ Now tell the groups that they have to create a simple mime and provide a commentary to it. For example: getting out of bed and getting dressed; filling the kettle and making a cup of tea; coming into a room and snatching the packet of crisps from a little brother's hands. Explain that the mime must be brief and uncomplicated. Give the groups five minutes to prepare.

⊛ Ask some students to share their work and ask the class to comment on how well the commentary links with the action. How does the commentator create the sense of occasion or atmosphere?

Follow up

⊛ Provide some video footage without sound for students to use.

First you need...

Objective covered
S&L9 *Recognise the way familiar spoken texts, e.g. directions, explanations, are organised and identify their typical features, e.g. of vocabulary or tone.*

Aim
To revise the importance of imperative verbs and sequencing connectives when giving instructions or directions.

Activity

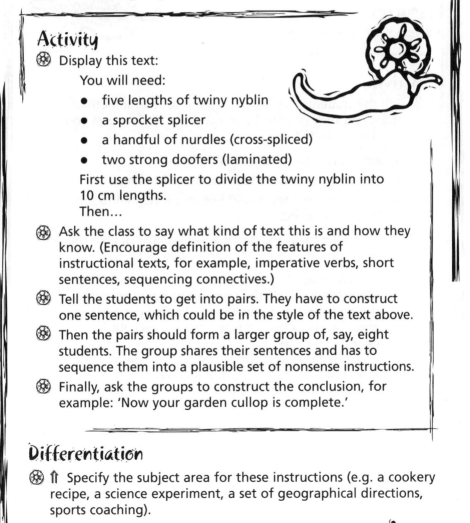

- ⊛ Display this text:

    You will need:
    - five lengths of twiny nyblin
    - a sprocket splicer
    - a handful of nurdles (cross-spliced)
    - two strong doofers (laminated)

    First use the splicer to divide the twiny nyblin into 10 cm lengths.
    Then…

- ⊛ Ask the class to say what kind of text this is and how they know. (Encourage definition of the features of instructional texts, for example, imperative verbs, short sentences, sequencing connectives.)

- ⊛ Tell the students to get into pairs. They have to construct one sentence, which could be in the style of the text above.

- ⊛ Then the pairs should form a larger group of, say, eight students. The group shares their sentences and has to sequence them into a plausible set of nonsense instructions.

- ⊛ Finally, ask the groups to construct the conclusion, for example: 'Now your garden cullop is complete.'

Differentiation

- ⊛ ⇑ Specify the subject area for these instructions (e.g. a cookery recipe, a science experiment, a set of geographical directions, sports coaching).

Listen carefully

YEAR 8

Objective covered
S&L7 *Listen for a specific purpose, paying sustained attention and selecting for comment or question that which is relevant to the agreed focus.*

Aim
To focus students' listening skills on a specific topic.

Resources
Individual whiteboards and pens.

Activity

* Tell the students that you are going to read something to them and they have to listen carefully. Explain that you want them to tell you:

  * what the topic of the reading is
  * one thing they have learned from listening
  * one question they would like to ask related to what they have heard.

* Now read the following passage – or another of your choice. This passage comes from *Mother Tongue* by Bill Bryson:

  > According to Mary Helen Dohan, in *Our Own Words*, the military vehicle the tank got its name because during its secretive experimental phase people were encouraged to think it was a storage receptacle – hence a tank. The curiously nautical terminology for its various features – hatch, turret, hull, deck – arises from the fact that it was developed by the British Admiralty rather than the Army.

* Share responses (orally or on whiteboards).

Differentiation

* ⇓ Read the passage twice.

  ⇑ Use a longer passage if you have a high-attaining group.

Lights, camera, action!

Objective covered / aim

S&L14 *Convey action, character, atmosphere and tension when scripting and performing plays.*

Activity

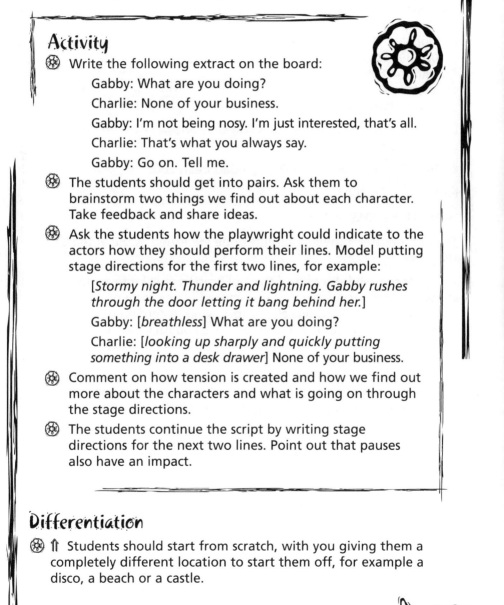

⊛ Write the following extract on the board:

> Gabby: What are you doing?
>
> Charlie: None of your business.
>
> Gabby: I'm not being nosy. I'm just interested, that's all.
>
> Charlie: That's what you always say.
>
> Gabby: Go on. Tell me.

⊛ The students should get into pairs. Ask them to brainstorm two things we find out about each character. Take feedback and share ideas.

⊛ Ask the students how the playwright could indicate to the actors how they should perform their lines. Model putting stage directions for the first two lines, for example:

> [*Stormy night. Thunder and lightning. Gabby rushes through the door letting it bang behind her.*]
>
> Gabby: [*breathless*] What are you doing?
>
> Charlie: [*looking up sharply and quickly putting something into a desk drawer*] None of your business.

⊛ Comment on how tension is created and how we find out more about the characters and what is going on through the stage directions.

⊛ The students continue the script by writing stage directions for the next two lines. Point out that pauses also have an impact.

Differentiation

⊛ ⇑ Students should start from scratch, with you giving them a completely different location to start them off, for example a disco, a beach or a castle.

Published by Letts Educational
The Chiswick Centre
414 Chiswick High Road
London W4 5TF
☎ 020 89963333
✆ 020 87428390
✉ mail@lettsed.co.uk
🖳 www.letts-education.com

Letts Educational Limited is a division of Granada Learning Limited, part of Granada plc.

© Simon Adorian, Beth Brooke, Lyn Gaudreau 2002

First published 2002

ISBN 184085 7048

The authors assert the moral right to be identified as the authors of this work.

British Library Cataloguing in Publication Data
A catalogue record for this book is available from the British Library.

Commissioned by Helen Clark
Project management by Vicky Butt
Editing by June Hall and Mark Haslam
Cover design by Ken Vail Graphic Design
Internal design by IFA Design Ltd
Illustrations by IFA Design Ltd
Production by PDQ
Printed and bound by Ashford Colour Press